Traditional
HOME PLANS

GARLINGHOUSE

Library of Congress No: 88-82799

ISBN: 0-938708-22-8

Canadian orders should be submitted to:

The Garlinghouse Company, Inc.
20 Cedar Street North
Kitchener, Ontario N2H 2W8
(519) 743-4169

TABLE OF CONTENTS

059701 ✓
4.95PB

Sun Space Warms To Entertaining

No. 10495

Tile is used to soak up solar heat in the sun space and also to add a tailored accent to the total home arrangement. Leading from the air-lock entry toward the living room spaces of this marvelous home, the tile separates the activity areas from the sleeping quarters. With two bedrooms on the second story, the lower area includes the master bedroom suite with its divided bath and walk-in closet. The utilitarian areas of the home are also enhanced by direct access to the sun space plus a space-stretching central island.

First floor — 1,691 sq. ft.
Second floor — 512 sq. ft.
Garage — 484 sq. ft.
Sun space — 108 sq. ft.
Basement — 1,691 sq. ft.

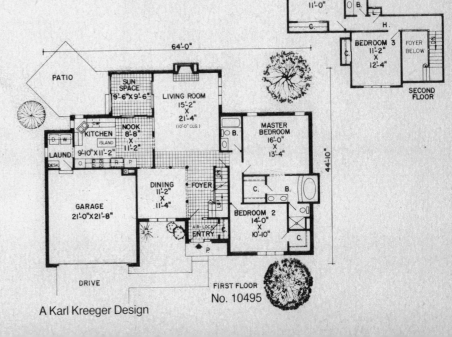

A Karl Kreeger Design

Master Retreat Crowns Spacious Home

No. 19422

Here's a compact beauty with a wide-open feeling. Step past the inviting front porch, and savor a breathtaking view of active areas: the columned entry with its open staircase and windows high overhead; the soaring living room, divided from the kitchen and dining room by the towering fireplace chimney; the screened porch beyond the triple living room windows. Tucked behind the stairs, you'll find a cozy parlor. And, across the hall, a bedroom with an adjoining full bath features access to the screened porch. Upstairs, the master suite is an elegant retreat you'll want to come home for, with its romantic dormer window seat, private balcony, and double-vanitied bath.

First floor — 1,290 sq. ft.
Second floor — 405 sq. ft.
Screened porch — 152 sq. ft.
Garage — 513 sq. ft.

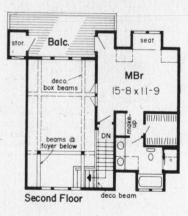

Second Floor

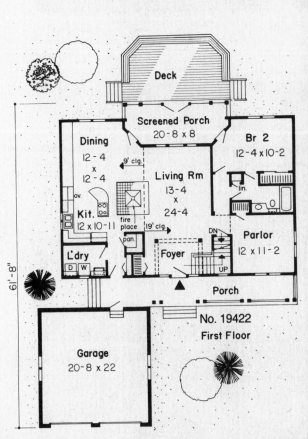

Deck

Screened Porch
20-8 x 8

Dining
12-4
x
12-4

9' clg.

ov.

Kit.
12 x 10-11

fire place

pan.

19' clg.

L'dry
D W

Living Rm
13-4
x
24-4

lin.

Br 2
12-4 x 10-2

DN

Foyer

UP

Parlor
12 x 11-2

Porch

61'-8"

Garage
20-8 x 22

No. 19422
First Floor

The Best of Old and New

No. 90710

If you long for a family home that combines the beauty of Victorian design with the amenities of a modern plan, look no further. Old-fashioned touches include a gingerbread exterior complete with romantic verandas on two floors, a two-story bay that adds wonderful angles and a spacious feeling to the formal parlor and the master bedroom, and a cozy, fireplaced gathering room at the rear of the house. But, don't overlook the strategic location of the kitchen, just steps away from the formal dining room, or the elegant bath with the convenience of both a tub and walk-in shower. There's even a screened porch at the rear of the house, a perfect place for rainy day play.

First floor — 1,068 sq. ft.
Second floor — 868 sq. ft.

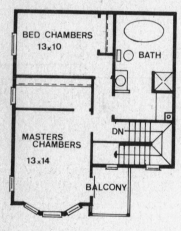

BED CHAMBERS
13×10

BATH

MASTERS
CHAMBERS
13×14

DN

BALCONY

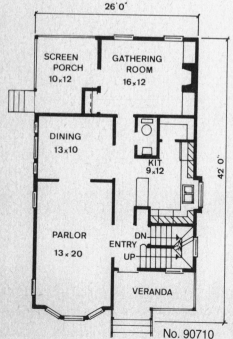

26'0"

SCREEN
PORCH
10×12

GATHERING
ROOM
16×12

DINING
13×10

KIT
9×12

42'0"

PARLOR
13×20

DN
ENTRY
UP

VERANDA

No. 90710

Traditional Warmth

No. 10806

With its abundant windows and covered porch, this traditional Tudor masterpiece boasts an atmosphere that says "welcome." Show your guests into the sunken living room just off the entry, or the adjoining dining room at the rear of the house. With the efficient island kitchen just steps away, the cook's job will be easy. When the gathering's informal, the adjoining fireplaced great room, which features access to both a screened porch and outdoor deck, is a comfortable alternative. Guests will appreciate the first-floor powder room just around the corner. A graceful staircase leads to three ample bedrooms, each with a walk-in closet, one optional sitting room-bedroom, and two full baths.

First floor — 1,469 sq. ft.
Second floor — 1,241 sq. ft.
Garage — 3-car

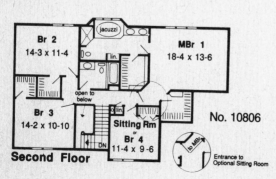

Second Floor — No. 10806

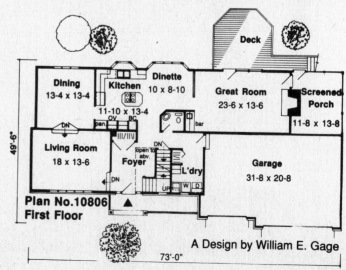

Plan No. 10806 First Floor

A Design by William E. Gage

Master Suite Crowns Outstanding Plan

No. 10334

Here's a fabulous executive home. Incorporating a study, walk-in closet, and lavish bath with whirlpool, shower, and skylight, the master suite adds a finishing touch to this exceptional home. The deck-edged main level details an eye-catching 25 ft. oak-floored great room with bow window. Also outlined are two bedrooms, a slate-floored dining room, and kitchen with pantry and snack island. On the basement level, the family room joins the patio via sliding glass doors, and a fourth bedroom and extra bath are included.

Main level — 1,742 sq. ft.
Upper level — 809 sq. ft.
Lower level — 443 sq. ft.
Basement — 1,270 sq. ft.
Garage — 558 sq. ft.

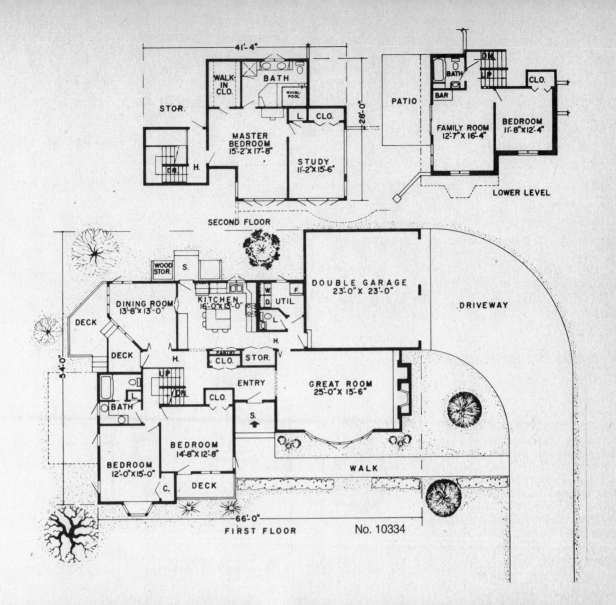

41'-4"

STOR.

WALK-IN CLO.

BATH

WHIRL-POOL

L.   CLO.

MASTER BEDROOM
15'-2" X 17'-8"

STUDY
11'-2" X 15'-6"

28'-0"

SECOND FLOOR

PATIO

BAR

BATH

CLO.

FAMILY ROOM
12'-7" X 16'-4"

BEDROOM
11'-8" X 12'-4"

LOWER LEVEL

WOOD STOR.

S.

DINING ROOM
13'-8" X 13'-0"

DECK

DECK

KITCHEN
16'-0" X 13'-0"

W   D   L

UTIL.

F.

DOUBLE GARAGE
23'-0" X 23'-0"

DRIVEWAY

H.

CLO.   STOR.

ENTRY

BATH

UP DN

CLO.

S.

GREAT ROOM
25'-0" X 15'-6"

54'-0"

BEDROOM
14'-8" X 12'-8"

BEDROOM
12'-0" X 15'-0"

C.

DECK

WALK

66'-0"

FIRST FLOOR   No. 10334

Veranda Brings Romance to Compact Plan

No. 20350

Two fireplaces add curbside appeal, and insure a toasty atmosphere in this three-bedroom Victorian charmer. The ample foyer opens to a sloping, sunken living room crowned by a towering chimney. Serve a formal meal in the adjoining dining room, or enjoy a cozy supper at the handy eating bar that separates the kitchen and family room. And, when the weather's nice, enjoy your after dinner coffee on the patio. The spacious bedrooms upstairs include the sunny master suite with its own private bath and built-in vanity. Another full bath serves the rear bedrooms.

First floor — 972 sq. ft.
Second floor — 821 sq. ft.
Basement — 972 sq. ft.

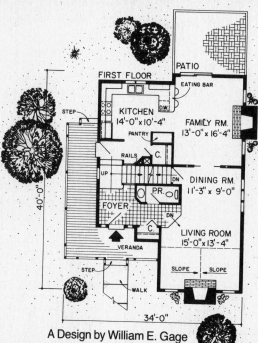

No. 20350

A Design by William E. Gage

Expansive Two Story Foyer Creates Dramatic Impression

No. 10588

French doors in the breakfast nook give this traditional colonial home a touch of romance. Divided from the kitchen by a peninsula with a counter for informal meals, the breakfast nook is adjacent to the fireplaced family room. Right across the hall, the foyer links living and dining rooms and harbors the angular staircase to four bedrooms and two baths on the second floor.

First floor — 1,450 sq. ft.
Second floor — 1,082 sq. ft.
Basement — 1,340 sq. ft.
Garage — 572 sq. ft.

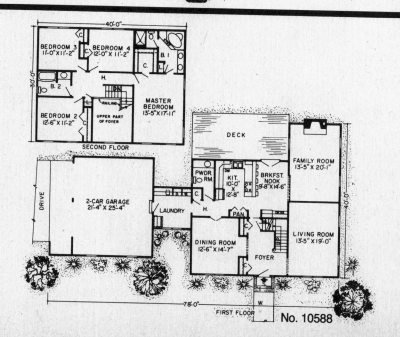

No. 10588

Double Doors Give Spanish Welcome

No. 10108

Massive double doors open to the foyer of this multi-arched Spanish design and balance three sets of double doors opening to a second floor balcony. Spanning over 27 feet, the living room occupies the entire area to the right of the foyer, while the kitchen and family room edge the left side. Hallway, bath, and laundry niche separate the areas and buffer noises. Three large bedrooms boast two baths.

First floor — 1,176 sq. ft.
Second floor — 1,176 sq. ft.
Basement — 1,176 sq. ft.
Garage — 576 sq. ft.

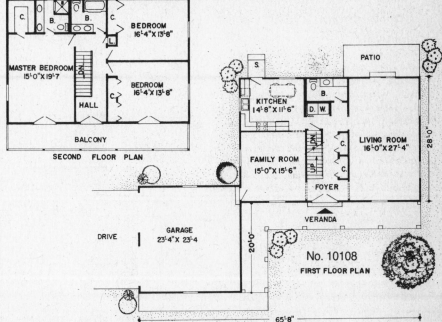

SECOND FLOOR PLAN

MASTER BEDROOM 15'-0" X 19'-7"
BEDROOM 16'-4" X 13'-8"
BEDROOM 16'-4" X 13'-8"
HALL
BALCONY

No. 10108
FIRST FLOOR PLAN

PATIO
KITCHEN 14'-8" X 11'-6"
FAMILY ROOM 15'-0" X 15'-6"
LIVING ROOM 16'-0" X 27'-4"
FOYER
VERANDA
GARAGE 23'-4" X 23'-4"
DRIVE
65'-8"
28'-0"
20'-0"

Enjoy the Backyard Views

No. 10550

There's lots of room for your growing family in this four bedroom Tudor beauty. Recessed ceilings in the dining room and master bedroom suite, a vaulted front office, and a beamed great room give first floor living areas distinctive angles. And, the sunporch off the breakfast nook is a warm place to curl up even on the coldest day. You'll never have to worry about traffic jams on busy weekday mornings. With two full baths upstairs and two convenient lavatories on the first floor, everyone can get out on time.

First floor — 2,069 sq. ft.
Second floor — 821 sq. ft.
Basement — 2,045 sq. ft.
Garage — 562 sq. ft.

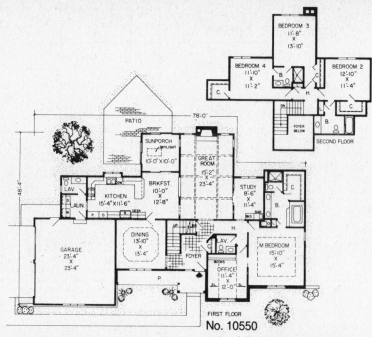

No. 10550

A Karl Kreeger Design

Classic Farmhouse

No. 10362

This house says "home" to everyone who remembers the bygone era but thinks ahead for comfort and values. The big wrap porch follows tradition. Imagine the cool summer evenings spent there. A split landing stairway leads to the four bedrooms on the upper level, complete with two bathrooms and lots of closets, perfect for the growing family. On the main level a wood-burning, built-in fireplace in the living room adds to the nostalgic charm of this home. Sliding glass doors open onto the porch. The main level also boasts a den, lavatory, utility room, kitchen and separate dining room overlooking the porch. An enclosed breezeway connects the double garage to the house.

Main level — 1,104 sq. ft.
Upper level — 1,124 sq. ft.
Basement — 1,080 sq. ft.
Garage — 528 sq. ft.

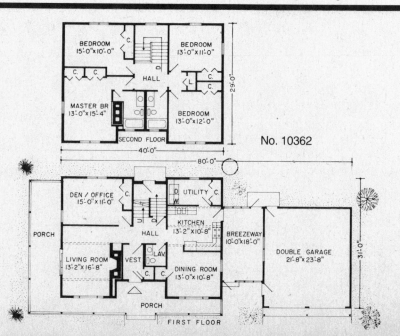

No. 10362

Rural Farmhouse Profile

No. 26001

A varied gabled roof, a large railed front porch and wood create a picturesque rural farmhouse profile in this plan. On the lower level a central hallway channels traffic easily to all rooms — a spaciouus formal living room and family-dining area with a bay window and fireplace in the front, and a bedroom suite, utility area, and kitchen at the back. A mud room is suitably located adjacent to the utility area. A sheltered outside entrance to the utility room and the double garage is given by a breeze-way-porch. On the second level three bedrooms nearly encircle a center bath.

First floor — 1,184 sq. ft.
Second floor — 821 sq. ft.
Basement — 821 sq. ft.
Garage — 576 sq. ft.
Front porch — 176 sq. ft.
Side porch — 69 sq. ft.

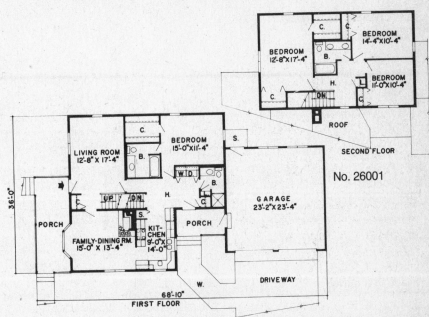

No. 26001

Kitchen Is Gourmet's Heaven

No. 10417

Inside and out, this design speaks of space and luxury. Outside, cedar shake roofing contrasts nicely with brick veneer to compliment arched and leaded windows and false dormers. Double entry doors usher you into a two-story entrance with staircase curving gently to second level rooms. Ten-foot ceilings throughout the lower level and nine-foot ceilings upstairs add to the spaciousness already created by large rooms. And, look at these kitchen features — 60 sq. ft. of counter space, a 5 x 6 step-saving island cooking range, a desk area, a windowed eating nook, and nearby patio access.

First floor — 3,307 sq. ft.
Second floor — 837 sq. ft.
Garage — 646 sq. ft.
Porch and patios — 382 sq. ft.

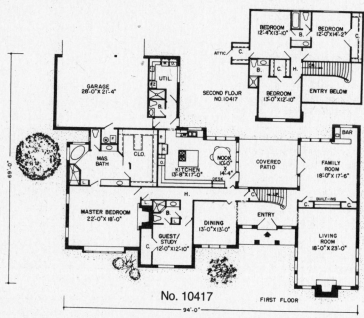

No. 10417

Extraordinary Exterior Draws Attention

No. 10442

Reminiscent of lordly manor houses, this home also features many more contemporary pleasures such as a sunken master bedroom with dressing areas; the outdoor enjoyment provided by decks, porches and patios; and a second story bridge overlooking the cathedral-ceilinged living room. Featuring 2,069 sq. ft. of well-organized living space on the first floor and 860 sq. ft. in the upper story, this splendid residence is desinged with two bedrooms and a game room on the second story. The game room is accented by a wetbar and its own fireplace.

First floor — 2,069 sq. ft.
Second floor — 860 sq. ft.
Garage — 600 sq. ft.

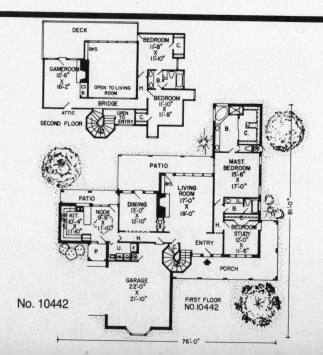

No. 10442

14

Perfect for Parties

No. 10663

Does your family enjoy entertaining? Here's your home! This handsome, rambling beauty can handle a crowd of any size. Greet your guests in a beautiful foyer that opens to the cozy, bayed living room and elegant dining room with floor-to-ceiling windows. Show them the impressive two-story gallery and book-lined study, flooded with sunlight from atrium doors and clerestory windows. Or, gather around the fire in the vaulted family room. The bar connects to the efficient kitchen, just steps away from both nook and formal dining room. And, when the guests go home, you'll appreciate your luxurious first-floor master suite and the cozy upstairs bedroom suites with adjoining sitting room.

First floor — 2,446 sq. ft.
Second floor — 844 sq. ft.
Garage — 660 sq. ft.

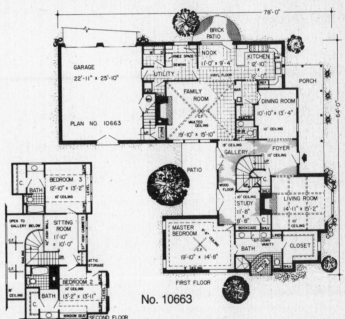

No. 10663

Eating Options Offered

No. 10421

The kitchen's location next to the nook and dining room, and only steps away from the covered patio, offers numerous options for both formal and informal dining. The kitchen is well-planned to save steps during food preparation, yet roomy enough for someone who likes to spread out. The dining area, which can be shut off from the kitchen by way of wood folding doors, is sunken 6 inches and lit with natural light from six 6 ft. windows. Glass variations across the front exterior also include arched gameroom windows, three arched windows in the master suite which form a box type bay, three 7'6" living room leaded windows and leaded skylight and transom at entry.

First floor — 1,605 sq. ft.
Second floor — 732 sq. ft.
Garage — 525 sq. ft.
Patio — 395 sq. ft.

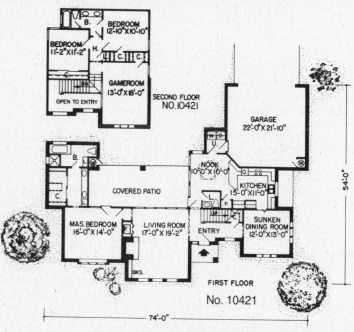

Large Covered Patio for Outdoor Enjoyment

No. 10436

Beauty and character flow from every area of this design. The double entry, set off by brickwork arches, ushers you into a large foyer with a curving staircase. The family room and fireplaced living room share a bar and with the patio, are sunken 12 inches lower than the adjoining rooms. On yet a third level are the utility room and garage which lie up 12 inches. In addition to the lower level master suite, three additional bedrooms are located upstairs and complete the sleeping accommodations. Each bedroom has direct access to a bath, and the largest of the three boasts a bay window and adjoining library.

First floor — 2,277 sq. ft.
Second floor — 851 sq. ft.
Garage — 493 sq. ft.

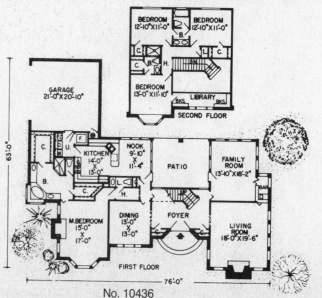

Morning Room Adds Gracious Accent

No. 10445

Tiled floors unify the dining and food preparation areas of this masterful design. Located off the well-organized kitchen is a morning room that's perfect for an elegant brunch or some private time before the day begins. Highlighted by a solarium, this octagonal room opens onto the centrally located living room that features built-in bookcases, a fireplace and a wetbar. The family room design employs more tile accents and opens onto the patio. The secluded master bedroom suite features a sunken tub, a small greenhouse for the plant enthusiast and roomy closets.

First floor — 2,466 sq. ft.
Garage — 482 sq. ft.

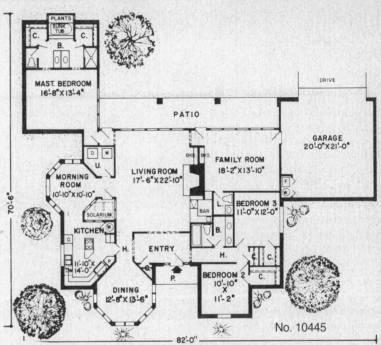

PLANTS
SUNK TUB
C.   B.   C.

MAST. BEDROOM
16'-8" X 13'-4"

DRIVE

PATIO

GARAGE
20'-0" X 21'-0"

D W

U.

MORNING
ROOM
10'-10" X 10'-10"

LIVING ROOM
17'-6" X 22'-10"

BKS BKS

FAMILY ROOM
18'-2" X 13'-10"

F
W

SOLARIUM

KITCHEN
W

BAR

L.

B.

BEDROOM 3
11'-0" X 12'-0"

70'-6"

11'-10" X
14'-0"

DW
P

H.

ENTRY

H.

C. C.

DINING
12'-8" X 13'-6"

P.

BEDROOM 2
10'-10"
X
11'-2"

C. C.

82'-0"

No. 10445

Two-Way Fireplace Warms Living Areas

No. 10652

Stucco, fieldstone, and rough-hewn timbers grace the elegant exterior of this three-bedroom family home. But with abundant windows, high ceilings, and an open plan, this cheerful abode is a far cry from the chilly Tudor castle of long ago. Flanked by a vaulted formal dining room and a stairway to the upstairs bedrooms, full bath, and built-in cedar closet, the central foyer leads to a spacious living room, kept comfortable in any season by a ceiling fan. Nearby, the first-floor master suite is loaded with amenities: a walk-in closet, skylit double vanities, and a sunken tub. Notice the cooktop island convenience in the kitchen, the built-in bar adjacent to the living room, and the rear deck accessible through French doors in the breakfast room.

First floor — 1,789 sq. ft.
Second floor — 568 sq. ft.
Basement — 1,789 sq. ft.
Garage — 529 sq. ft.

No. 10652

A Karl Kreeger Design

Victorian Details Enhance Facade

No. 10593

A charming porch shelters the entrance of this four bedroom home with a country kitchen. In colder climates, the closed vestibule cuts heat loss. Off the central foyer, the cozy living room shares a fireplace with the family room, which contains a bar and access to the patio and screened porch for entertaining. The bay-windowed breakfast room is handy for quick meals. Or, use the formal dining room with octagonal recessed ceiling. All the bedrooms, located on the second floor, have walk-in closets.

First floor — 1,450 sq. ft.
Second floor — 1,341 sq. ft.
Basement — 1,450 sq. ft.
Garage — 629 sq. ft.
Covered porch — 144 sq. ft.
Wood storage — 48 sq. ft.

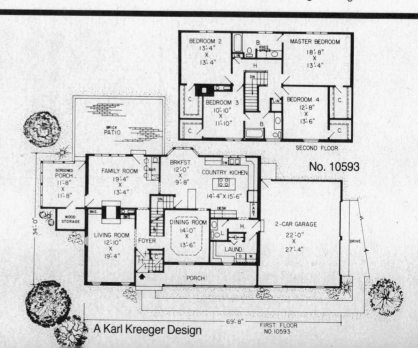

No. 10593

A Karl Kreeger Design

Open-Beamed Ceilings Offered In Plan

No. 10573

Expansive beautiful ceilings are offered in this spacious design. The exterior is built with a brick and stucco frontage and wood veneer siding on the side and rear elevations. It also has a shake shingle roof. On the first floor, a large foyer is available with closet space. From the foyer and to the left lie the living and dining rooms. The living room has a large bay window. The dining room is more formal and has a decorative raised ceiling. From the dining room lies the kitchen with its own pantry, a beautiful open-beamed ceiling, and a bay-windowed breakfast nook. Another feature of the first floor is the sunken family room that has a large wood-burning fireplace and massive open beams hanging from its ceiling.

First floor — 1,306 sq. ft.
Second floor — 1,248 sq. ft.
Basement — 1,338 sq. ft.
Garage — 540 sq. ft.

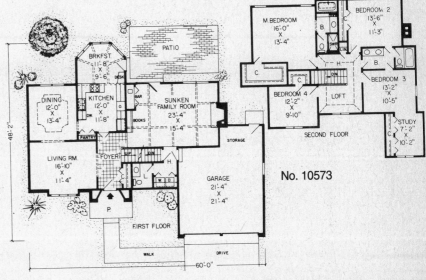

No. 10573

A Karl Kreeger Design

Cape Cod Passive Solar Design

No. 10386

A solar greenhouse on the south employs energy storage rods and water to capture the sun's warmth, thereby providing a sanctuary for plants and supplying a good percentage of the house's heat. Other southern windows are large and triple glazed for energy efficiency. From one of the bedrooms, located on the second floor, you can look out through louvered shutters to the living room below, accented by a heat circulating fireplace and a cathedral ceiling with three dormer windows which flood the room with light. On the lower level, sliding glass doors lead from the sitting area of the master bedroom suite to a private patio. Also on this level are a dining room, kitchen, mud room, double garage with a large storage area and another larger patio.

First floor — 1,164 sq. ft.
Second floor — 574 sq. ft.
Basement — 1,164 sq. ft.
Greenhouse — 238 sq. ft.
Garage & storage — 566 sq. ft.

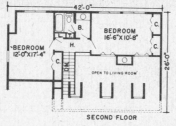

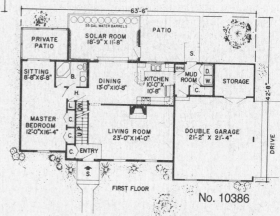

Colonial Detailing Enlivens Exterior

No. 10020

Impressive Colonial columns punctuate the semi-circular porch and fuse with the bow windows and brick to create an exceptional facade. Inside, the floor plan is a study in modern living. Fireplaces grace both the living room and the family room, which opens to an expansive terrace. A formal dining room adjoins the highly functional kitchen, and the 21-foot master bedroom boasts a lavish full bath and double closets. Two front bedrooms are accented with lovely bow windows.

First floor — 2,512 sq. ft.
Basement — 2,512 sq. ft.
Garage — 648 sq. ft.

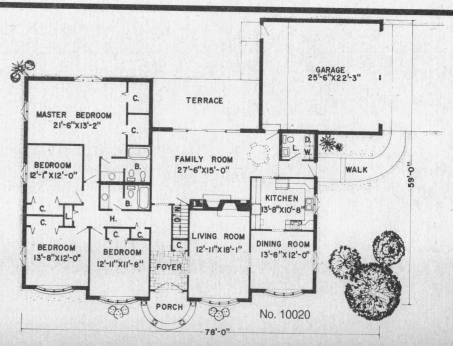

Garden Room Brings the Outdoors In

No. 10423

This floor plan flows with unmatched character throughout its entirety. Spiral stairs, leading to a bay-windowed second floor loft, catch your eye as you enter. Highlighting the quieter living areas is the master bedroom suite. A fireplace and split his and her closet and bath area with sunken tub is found here. Sharing two of its inside walls of windows with the eight-sided eating nook and fireplaced living room, the garden room can become your haven for plants as well as a focus of interest of the home.

First floor — 2,506 sq. ft.
Loft — 267 sq. ft.
Garage — 521 sq. ft.
Patio & porch — 155 sq. ft.

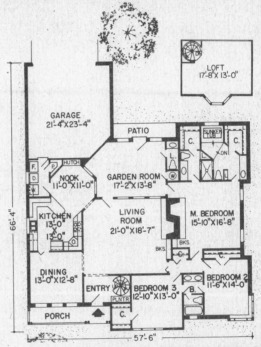

LOFT 17'-8" X 13'-0"

GARAGE 21'-4" X 23'-4"

PATIO

SUNKEN TUB

NOOK 11'-0" X 11'-0"

GARDEN ROOM 17'-2" X 13'-8"

M. BEDROOM 15'-10" X 16'-8"

KITCHEN 13'-0" X 13'-0"

LIVING ROOM 21'-0" X 18'-7"

HUTCH

DINING 13'-0" X 12'-8"

ENTRY

BEDROOM 3 12'-10" X 13'-0"

BEDROOM 2 11'-6" X 14'-0"

PORCH

66'-4"

57'-6"

No. 10423

French Charmer Features Two-story Foyer and Great Room

No. 10529

The second floor incorporates three bedrooms and two baths, with the hall overlooking both the great room and the foyer. The master bedroom and bath are on the first floor. The expansive great room includes a bar, a fireplace and opens onto the patio. The kitchen is convenient to the dining room, breakfast room and walk-in pantry.

First floor — 1,634 sq. ft.
Second floor — 879 sq. ft.
Basement — 1,634 sq. ft.
Garage — 491 sq. ft.

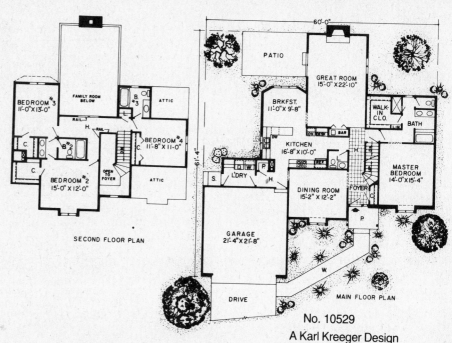

No. 10529
A Karl Kreeger Design

Compact, but Elegant

No. 20077

You'll never get bored with the rooms in this charming, three-bedroom Victorian. The angular plan gives every room an interesting shape. From the wrap-around veranda, the entry foyer leads through the living room and parlor, breaking them up without confining them, and giving each room an airy atmosphere. In the dining room, with its hexagonal recessed ceiling, you can enjoy your after-dinner coffee and watch the kids playing on the deck. Or eat in the sunny breakfast room off the island kitchen, where every wall has a window, and every window has a different view. You'll love the master suite's bump-out windows, walk-in closets, and double sinks.

First floor — 1,393 sq. ft.
Second floor — 1,096 sq. ft.
Basement — 1,393 sq. ft.
Garage — 491 sq. ft.

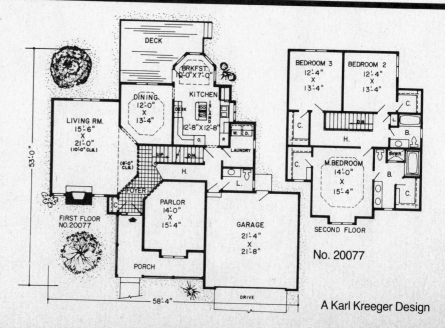

No. 20077

A Karl Kreeger Design

Bridge Over Foyer
Introduces Unique Features

No. 10535

A dynamic foyer opens into a cathedral-ceiling great room, complete with a cozy fireplace framed on both sides with bookshelves. The unique octagonal breakfast nook is tucked into a spacious kitchen with a view of back yard. The master bedroom boasts a quaint, but roomy, sitting room. Three full baths and two half baths are conveniently located for family and guests.

First floor — 2,335 sq. ft.
Second floor — 1,157 sq. ft.
Basement — 2,281 sq. ft.
Garage — 862 sq. ft.

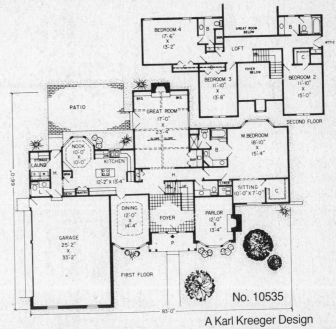

No. 10535

A Karl Kreeger Design

Private Court With Hot Tub Outside Master Bedroom

No. 10534

The luxury master suite is secluded on the first floor. Elegant touches include a library, morning room with built-ins, a bar with wine storage, and a sun porch with French doors into the dining room. The living room and foyer rise to the second floor which is comprised of three large bedrooms and two well-placed baths.

First floor — 2,486 sq. ft.
Second floor — 892 sq. ft.
Basement — 2,486 sq. ft.
Garage — 576 sq. ft.

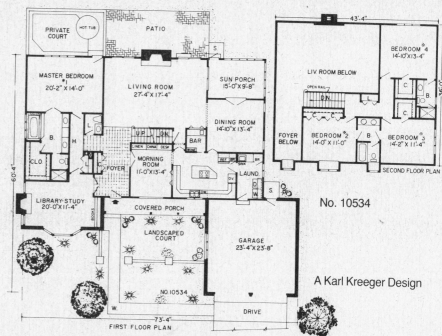

A Karl Kreeger Design

Master Suite Features Cozy Hearth

No. 10635

Columns adorn the classic entry of this traditional colonial dwelling. A hallway, flanked by the living room and beamed family room with fireplace, leads directly into the convenient island kitchen. Eat in the formal dining room or sunny dinette. Sliding glass doors lead to the patio for outside entertaining. Four bedrooms and two baths lie at the top of the central staircase.

First floor — 1,280 sq. ft.
Second floor — 1,224 sq. ft.
Basement — 1,283 sq. ft.
Garage — 576 sq. ft.

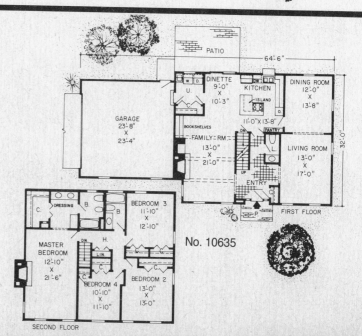

Bay Windows and Skylights Brighten this Tudor Home

No. 10673

Step from the arched fieldstone porch into the two-story foyer, and you can see that this traditional four bedroom home possesses a wealth of modern elements. Behind double doors lie the library and fireplaced living room, bathed in sunlight from two skylights in the sloping roof. Step out to the brick patio from the laundry room or bay-windowed breakfast room. For ultimate relaxation, the master bedroom suite contains a whirlpool tub. One bedroom boasts bay windows; another features a huge walk-in closet over the two car garage.

First floor — 1,265 sq. ft.
Second floor — 1,210 sq. ft.
Basement — 1,247 sq. ft.
Garage — 506 sq. ft.

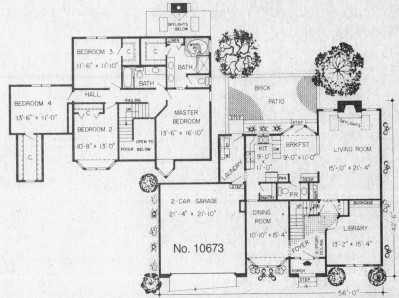

A Karl Kreeger Design

Outstanding Luxury Design is Always Popular

No. 10531

Here's a stately home that's a treasure chest of popular features, including a sunken great room, a spectacular breakfast nook, and a bridge-like balcony on the 2nd floor. The luxurious, 1st floor master suite is a marvel, with two huge walk-in closets, a 5-piece bath, and a sitting room with bay window. The 2nd and 3rd bedrooms each have a walk-in closet and private bath. The great room features a bar, fireplace, and built-in cabinets for TV and stereo, all crowned by a sloping, beamed ceiling. Both the dining room and the foyer have cathedral ceilings and are overlooked by the 2nd floor balcony. A fully equipped kitchen enjoys a sweeping view of the patio and opens to the stunning nook. All in all, this is a fabulous and impressive home.

First floor — 2,579 sq. ft.
Second floor — 997 sq. ft.
Basement — 2,579 sq. ft.
Garage & Storage — 1,001 sq. ft.

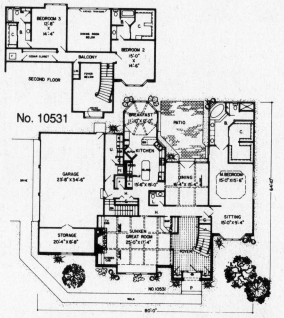

No. 10531

A Karl Kreeger Design

Tasteful Elegance Aim of Design

No. 22020

With an exterior that expresses French Provincial charm, this single level design emphasizes elegance and offers a semi-circular dining area overlooking the patio. To pamper parents, the master bedroom annexes a long dressing area and private bath, while another bath serves the second and third bedrooms. A wood-burning fireplace furnishes the family room.

Living area — 1,772 sq. ft.
Garage — 469 sq. ft.

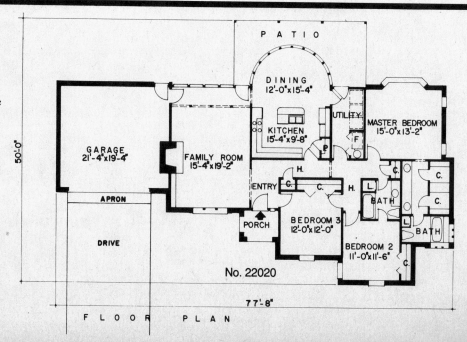

Central Chimney Serves Two Fireplaces

No. 10753

Convenience and elegance combine in this elegant brick Colonial. Entertaining? Formal areas flank the entry for the convenience of your guests. Close the dining room off from the bustle of the busy island kitchen without compromising efficiency. You'll be proud to show off the massive keeping room with its built-in wetbar and cozy fireplace. Three bedrooms lie up the open staircase, each with its own appealing features. The master suite includes double vanities, a step-in shower, and tub. The rear bedroom enjoys a view of the patio and a walk-in closet. The front bedroom boasts a bookcase wall. And, every room benefits from a chute that delivers dirty clothes right to the laundry room!

First floor — 1,671 sq. ft.
Second floor — 1,134 sq. ft.
Garage — 552 sq. ft.

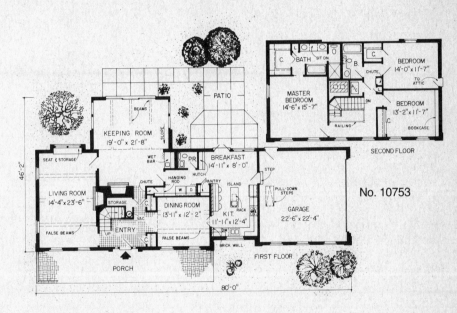

No. 10753

Stucco and Stone Reveal Outstanding Tudor Design

No. 10555

This beautiful stucco and stone masonry Tudor design opens to a formal foyer that leads through double doors into a well-designed library which is also conveniently accessible from the master bedroom. The master bedroom offers a vaulted ceiling and a huge bath area. Other features are an oversized living room with a fireplace, an open kitchen and a connecting dining room. A utility room and half bath are located next to a two-car garage. One other select option in this design is the separate cedar closet to use for off-season clothes storage.

First floor — 1,671 sq. ft.
Second floor — 505 sq. ft.
Basement — 1,661 sq. ft.
Garage — 604 sq. ft.
Screened porch — 114 sq. ft.

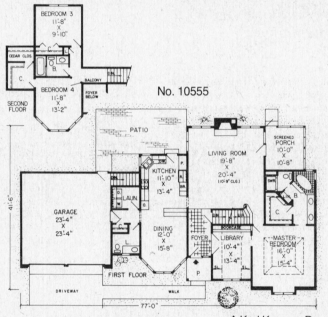

No. 10555

A Karl Kreeger Design

Elegant Master Suite Crowns Victorian

No. 20351

Gingerbread trim, round-top windows, and a two-story bay bring a Victorian flavor to this modern plan. A fireplace adds a cozy charm to the angular living room just off the foyer. Walk past the stairs and the handy powder room to the rear of the house. Flanked by the formal dining and family rooms, the convenient kitchen lets the cook enjoy family activities and prepare dinner, too! You'll appreciate the outdoor living space the rear deck adds. But, when there's a chill in the air, you can light a fire and enjoy the view from the window seat in the family room. Three upstairs bedrooms include the bayed master suite, which features loads of closet space, a raised whirlpool tub, and a step-in shower for busy mornings.

First floor — 1,304 sq. ft.
Second floor — 1,009 sq. ft.
Basement — 1,304 sq. ft.
Garage — 688 sq. ft.

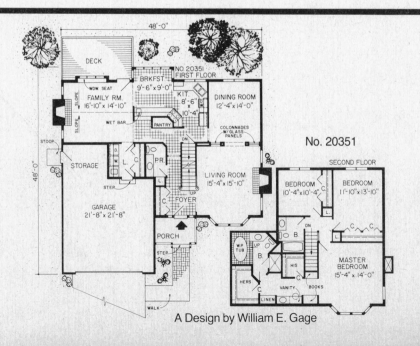

No. 20351

A Design by William E. Gage

28

A Stately Home

No. 9332

This charming English Tudor adaptation retains the appeal of yesteryear, yet features an outstanding contemporary floor plan. Three large bedrooms each have a closet over seven feet long. The living room has a fireplace, square bay window, and ornamental iron railing which runs along the stairway and entry. A formal dining room opens onto an elevated wood deck through sliding glass doors. The huge family room, which also has a fireplace, is located on the lower level.

Upper level — 1,633 sq. ft.
Lower level — 858 sq. ft.
Garage & shop — 718 sq. ft.

UPPER LEVEL

DECK

DINING ROOM 12'-6"X13'-0"

KITCHEN 11'-4"X13'-0"

BEDROOM 15'-0"X13'-0"

LIVING ROOM 18'-4"X16'-4"

ENTRY

BEDROOM 11'-6"X14'-4"

BEDROOM 11'-6"X12'-0"

52'-0"

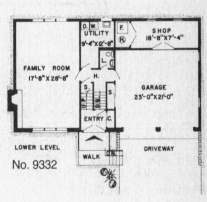

LOWER LEVEL

No. 9332

FAMILY ROOM 17'-8" X 28'-8"

UTILITY 9'-4"X12'-8"

SHOP 18'-8"X7'-4"

GARAGE 23'-0"X21'-0"

ENTRY

WALK

DRIVEWAY

Lots of Living in Four-bedroom Starter

No. 10520

This traditional exterior, with its charming dormers, provides four bedrooms and lots of style even on a small lot. The very large master suite on the second floor includes the luxury of a jacuzzi. The other second floor bedroom also has a private bath and a walk-in closet. On the first floor are two more bedrooms which share a bath. The living room is reminiscent of the old fashioned parlor. The dining area and U-shaped kitchen are located toward the back of the house overlooking the lawn and provide an ideal setting for family meals.

First floor — 960 sq. ft.
Second floor — 660 sq. ft.
Basement — 960 sq. ft.

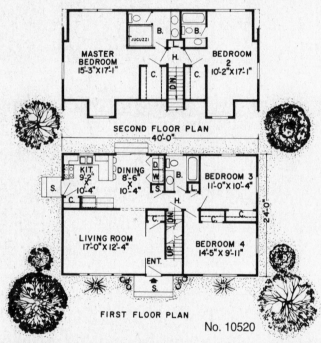

Roofed Walkway Attaches Garage

No. 9181

Placed behind the home and separate, so as not to detract from the rich traditional facade, the garage in this Colonial plan is attached by a roofed walkway. Brick and white pillars grace the exterior, while the interior floor plan speaks of modern luxury. The formal living room and dining room are placed to the left of the foyer, with the family room behind the living room having access to the terrace. To the right of the foyer are three bedrooms, one with a private bathroom.

Living area — 2,014 sq. ft.
Garage — 576 sq. ft.

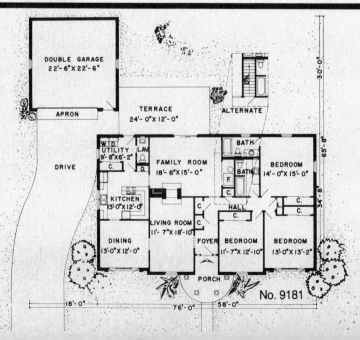

Stone Facade Accents Five-bedroom Home

No. 10530

Double-door entry leads to other first floor features including a hearth room with wood stove, window seat and built-in desk; master bedroom with fireplace, five-piece bath and private greenhouse entrance; multi-windowed great room with fireplace and deck access. Upstairs are four bedrooms, two baths, a study and a cedar closet.

First floor — 2,344 sq. ft.
Second floor — 1,382 sq. ft.
Basement — 2,344 sq. ft.
Garage — 781 sq. ft.
Shop — 286 sq. ft.

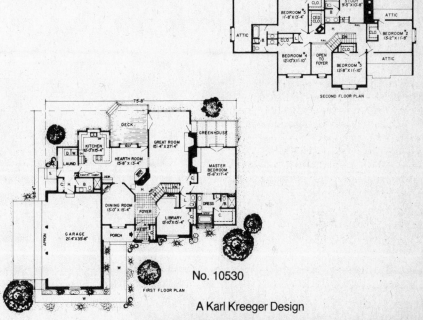

No. 10530

A Karl Kreeger Design

Passive Solar & Victorian Features Combine

No. 10382

The beauty of Victorian architecture and passive solar energy are combined in this attractive design. Scallops and laticework add distinction to the front exterior. Step inside and you'll find yourself in an air-lock entry which prevents the escape of heated air. A heat circulating, wood-burning fireplace adds charm to the living room besides providing warmth for the house in cold wintery weather.

First floor — 1,775 sq. ft.
Second floor — 1,296 sq. ft.
Basement — 1,763 sq. ft.
Greenhouse — 288 sq. ft.
Garage — 624 sq. ft.
Breezeway — 224 sq. ft.

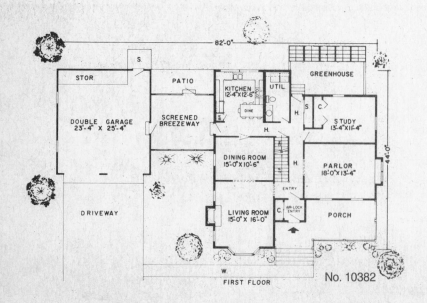

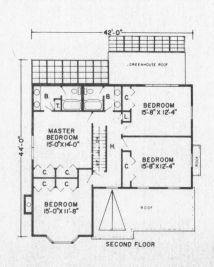

Book-lined Family Room

NO. 90117

Relax in this comfortable family room among the books and curl up in front of the fire. Or, on warmer days move through the glass doors and onto the patio which augments your living area. The formal living room and dining room are adjacent to the central foyer which incorporates a coat closet and a half bath for the convenience of guests. Family dining is accommodated by an area between the family room and the well planned kitchen. The second floor contains four bedrooms with the master bedroom having a double walk-in closet and a private bath. Linked to these rooms is an optional studio above the double garage.

First floor — 1,452 sq. ft.
Second floor — 1,158 sq. ft.
Optional studio — 264 sq. ft.

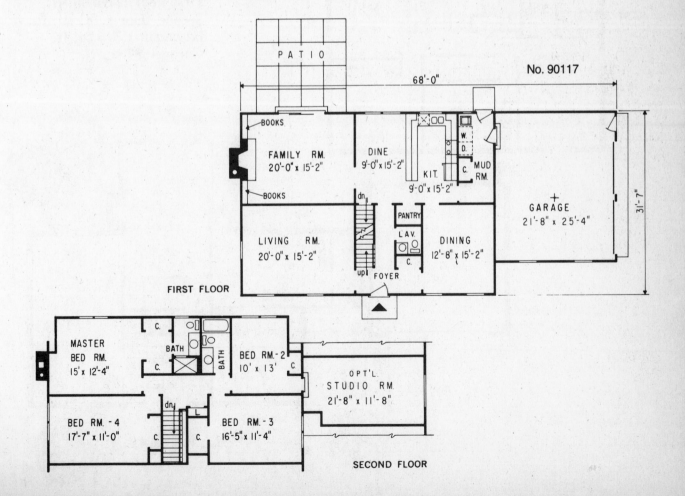

Southern Colonial Design

No. 10577

This southern colonial design of grand styling offers many oppulent features for homeowners. Stately exterior col- umns stand out from its brick exterior that also has a dash of wood veneer siding. Double doors lead to a spacious foyer which has closet space close by. Past the foyer is a half bath. To the right of the foyer is the living room and a family room. The family room has a wood-burning fireplace. To the left of the foyer is the dining room and the breakfast room. The kitchen is open to the breakfast room and to the left of the kitchen is the laundry room and the garage. The second level has four bedrooms and two full baths. Other ex- citing features of this design include the use of french doors that lead out to a brick patio from both the breakfast and the dining rooms.

First floor-1,490 sq. ft.
Second floor-1,183 sq. ft.
Basement-1,376 sq. ft.
Garage-537 sq. ft.

DRESSING
C.
B.
B.
DRESSING
LINEN
BEDROOM 4
10'-6" X 11'-6"
C.
H.
SECOND FLOOR
M.BEDROOM
12'-6" X 16'-6"
DN
BEDROOM 2
12'-4" X 10'-0"
BEDROOM 3
14'-0" X 11'-0"

GARAGE
21'-0" X 22'-0"
PATIO
FAMILY ROOM
13'-4" X 20'-0"
D. W.
LAUND.
KIT.
11'-0" X 11'-0"
BRKFST.
8'-0" X 13'-0"
LIVING ROOM
14'-0" X 25'-4"
40'-9"
P.
O.
R.
DINING RM.
14'-0" X 14'-0"
H.
L.
C.
DN
UP
FOYER
C.
C.
DRIVE
FIRST FLR.
NO.10577
PORCH
76'-0"

Colonial Classic

No. 10630

Are you a traditionalist? You'll love this graceful family home that incorporates the best of old and new by combining graceful colonial touches with modern zone design. Look at the detailing on the front door, the cozy hearth, the brick chimney, and covered patio leading to the garage. Then consider the convenient relationship between the kitchen and eat-ing areas. Notice how the utility room and adjoining lavatory off the patio makes returning from playtime or grocery shopping a breeze. Think of the convenience that two baths with double vanities will bring to your mornings. And, imagine how you'll enjoy escaping to the master suite to relax with a book in the sitting area or to take a lingering soak in the tub.

First floor — 1,360 sq. ft.
Second floor — 1,090 sq. ft.
Garage — 483 sq. ft.

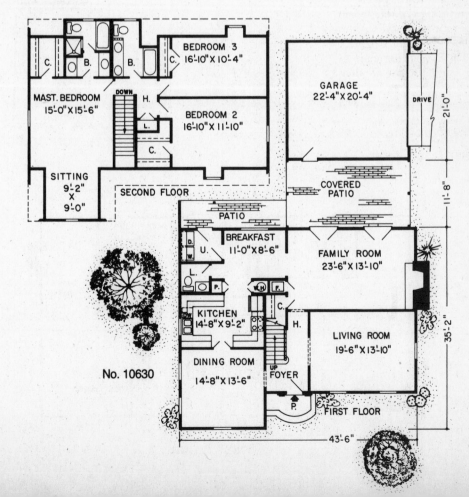

No. 10630

Country Charm Designed For Modern Living

No. 90157

The central two-story foyer with wrap-around balcony has access to a second floor front porch. The 22-foot family room with fireplace opens onto the rear patio. A country-sized kitchen features an adjacent breakfast area. The large master bedroom includes a deluxe bath with corner platform tub, angled vanity and separate shower. A spacious walk-in closet completes the master suite. A vaulted ceiling and half-circle window add to the charm of the front bedroom. Also featured is a two-car garage with plenty of storage space.

First floor—1,428 sq. ft.
Second floor—1,369 sq. ft.

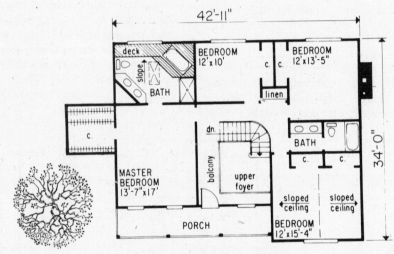

SECOND FLOOR

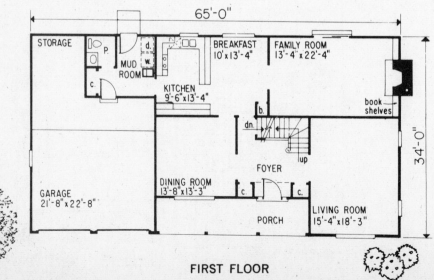

FIRST FLOOR

Clever Touches Improve Design

No. 20061

A lot can be said about this unique design. Its exterior of vertical siding, shake shingle and rock, and the large round picture window set this design apart. The interior is delightfully planned beginning with the kitchen that has a built-in pantry, refrigerator, dishwasher and range. In addition, the kitchen has a breakfast bar, an open-beamed ceiling with a skylight, plus a breakfast area with lots of windows. A very formal dining room is partitioned from the living room. The living room has two open beams running down a sloping ceiling, and a fireplace. There is a laundry closet and the foyer area also has a closet. Three bedrooms share a full bath. The master bedroom has an open-beamed, sloping ceiling with a spacious bath area and a walk-in closet.

First floor — 1,667 sq. ft.
Basement — 1,657 sq. ft.
Garage — 472 sq. ft.

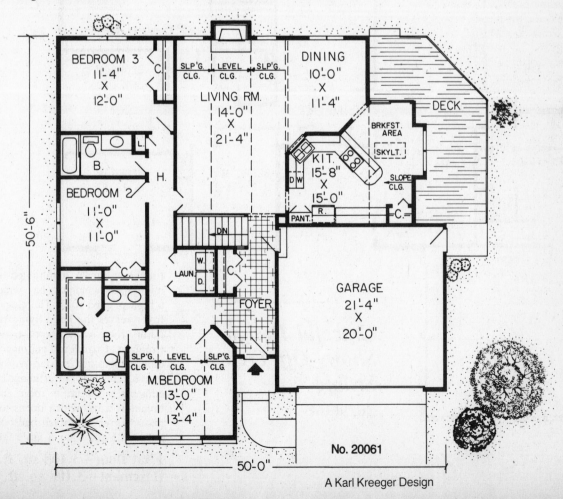

No. 20061

A Karl Kreeger Design

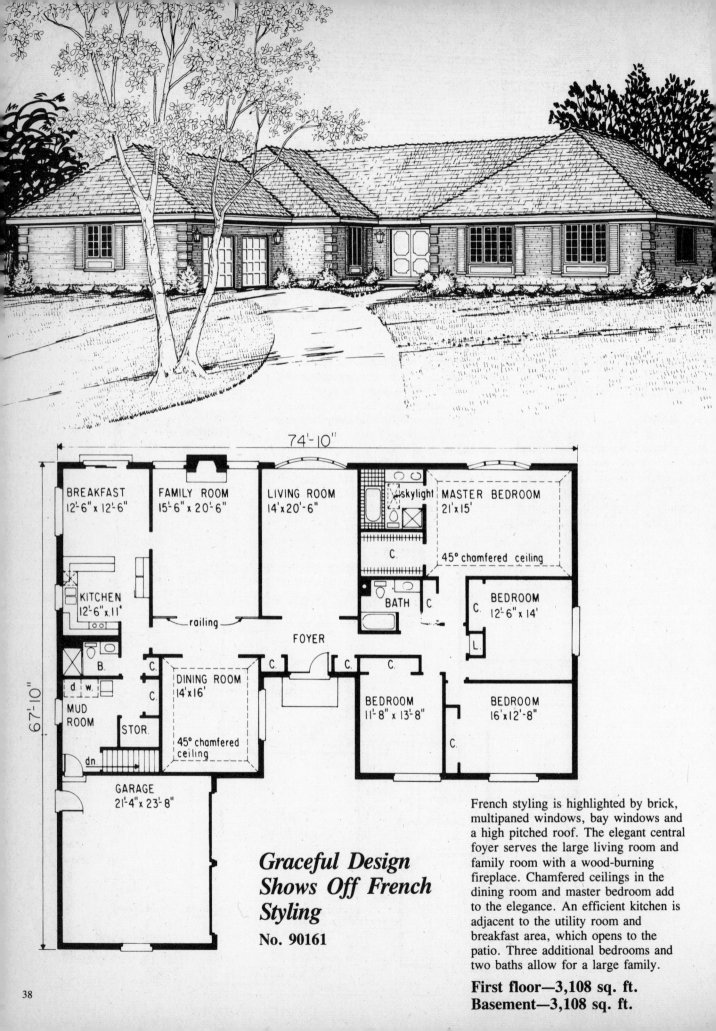

74'-10"

67'-10"

BREAKFAST
12'-6" x 12'-6"

FAMILY ROOM
15'-6" x 20'-6"

LIVING ROOM
14' x 20'-6"

skylight

MASTER BEDROOM
21' x 15'

45° chamfered ceiling

KITCHEN
12'-6" x 11'

C.

BATH

C.

railing

BEDROOM
12'-6" x 14'

C.

FOYER

B.

C.

C.

C.

C.

C.

d w

DINING ROOM
14' x 16'

BEDROOM
11'-8" x 13'-8"

BEDROOM
16' x 12'-8"

MUD ROOM

STOR.

45° chamfered ceiling

C.

dn

GARAGE
21'-4" x 23'-8"

Graceful Design Shows Off French Styling

No. 90161

French styling is highlighted by brick, multipaned windows, bay windows and a high pitched roof. The elegant central foyer serves the large living room and family room with a wood-burning fireplace. Chamfered ceilings in the dining room and master bedroom add to the elegance. An efficient kitchen is adjacent to the utility room and breakfast area, which opens to the patio. Three additional bedrooms and two baths allow for a large family.

First floor—3,108 sq. ft.
Basement—3,108 sq. ft.

Watch the World Go By

No. 90826

Rain or shine, the wrap-around porch on this Colonial classic is a perfect spot to put up your feet and relax. But, if you want more privacy, retreat to the rear patio instead. Inside, the inviting atmosphere continues in the huge living room with fieldstone fireplace and the island kitchen that opens to the family room. A cozy sewing room and study with full bath flank main living areas. The central staircase off the foyer leads to a massive master suite that shares the upper floor with two ample bedrooms and a third full bath.

First floor — 1,463 sq. ft.
Second floor — 981 sq. ft.
Basement — 814 sq. ft.

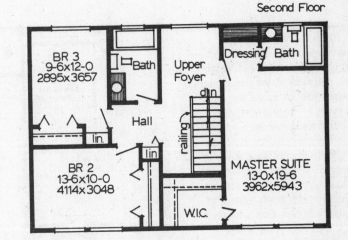

Second Floor

BR 3
9-6x12-0
2895x3657

Bath

Upper Foyer

Dressing   Bath

Hall

BR 2
13-6x10-0
4114x3048

railing

MASTER SUITE
13-0x19-6
3962x5943

lin.

W.I.C.

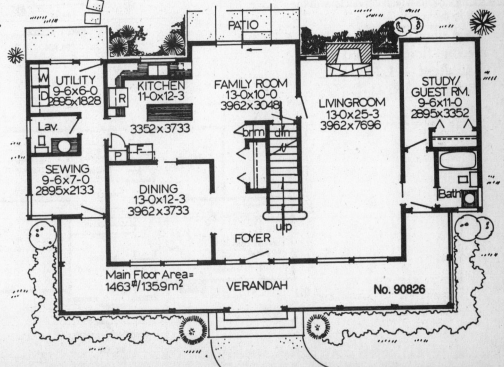

PATIO

UTILITY
9-6x6-0
2895x1828

KITCHEN
11-0x12-3

3352 x 3733

FAMILY ROOM
13-0x10-0
3962x3048

LIVINGROOM
13-0x25-3
3962x7696

STUDY/
GUEST RM.
9-6x11-0
2895x3352

Lav.

brm   dn

SEWING
9-6x7-0
2895x2133

P   F

DINING
13-0x12-3
3962x3733

Bath

FOYER

up

Main Floor Area=
1463 ⁿ/135.9m²

VERANDAH

No. 90826

Hand-hewn Timbers
In English Tudor

No. 90030

Once again, English architecture is enjoying wide popularity. There is something special about the dark hand-hewn timber and stone exterior, the paned and diamond-shaped windows, and the overall look that gives an impression of enduring comfort and security. Typical of this style is the open staircase which leads directly from the entrance foyer to the four bedrooms and open balcony on the second floor. A decorative metal circular staircase provides ready access to the upper balcony library that is located at the end of the living room, while directly behind is the beamed ceiling family room which connects with the outdoor terrace.

First floor — 1,565 sq. ft.
Second floor — 1,455 sq. ft.
Basement — 1,200 sq. ft.
Garage — 560 sq. ft.

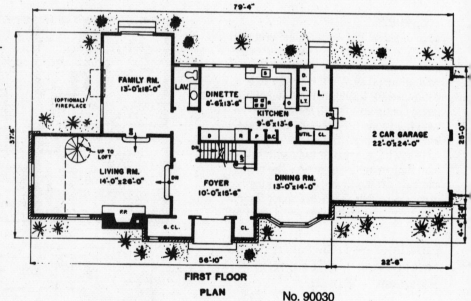

FIRST FLOOR PLAN   No. 90030

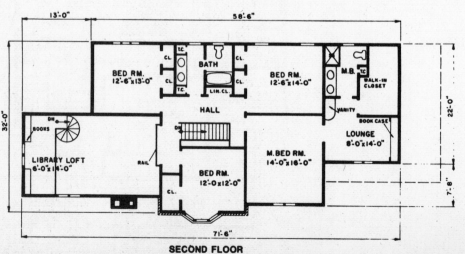

SECOND FLOOR PLAN

Gracious Design for Family Living

No. 90133

Designed for a family with children, this home contains four sizable bedrooms, a family room and outside terrace. Additional features include the beamed ceiling and optional fireplace in the family room, zoning of active and formal living areas, convenient location of the kitchen, and a mud room with first floor laundry. Unique in this home is the loft over the garage reached by disappearing stairs. This room makes an ideal hobby or game room. The overhanging second floor, clapboard siding and hay loft doors over the garage add up to an exterior that is unusual and definitely attractive.

First floor — 1,149 sq. ft.
Second floor — 988 sq. ft.

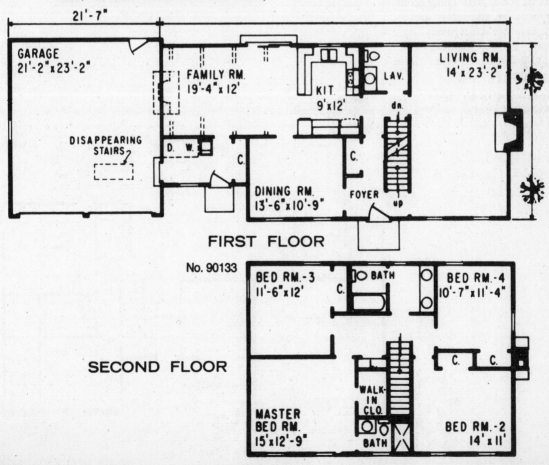

Bedroom Tower Creates Interesting Roof Line

No. 10618

Sloping ceilings and lofty open spaces are dominant features in this four-bedroom family home. Leading from the stairs to a full bath and two bedrooms, the upstairs hall is a bridge over the foyer and rustic living room. The dining room lies just off the foyer, adjacent to the island kitchen and breakfast room. The vaulted master suite with attached deck, a family bath, and bedroom with walk-in closet occupy a private wing.

First floor — 1,492 sq. ft.
Second floor — 475 sq. ft.
Garage — 413 sq. ft.

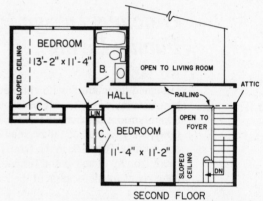

NO. 10618

A Karl Kreeger Design

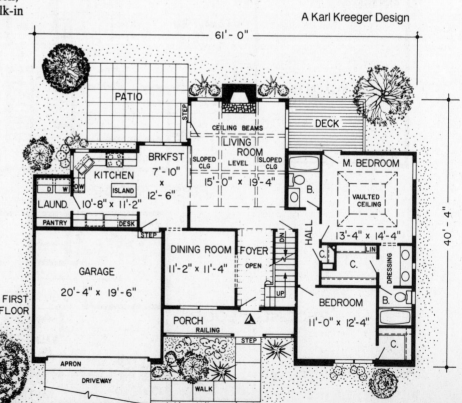

Warm and Inviting

No. 91209

The dormers that make the facade of this modified Cape so charming provide wonderful sitting nooks in the upstairs bedrooms. The kids will love the sloping ceilings and huge walk-in closets. You'll enjoy the warmth of a first-floor master suite with a fireplace. You'll appreciate the convenience of a U-shaped kitchen with a huge pantry, just steps away from formal and informal dining rooms. A screened porch means the kids can play outside, even on a rainy day. And, when guests arrive, show them to the living room off the foyer, or have them sit by the fire in the cozy family room.

First floor — 2,104 sq. ft.
Second floor — 1,147 sq. ft.
Basement — 1,946 sq. ft.
Screened porch — 326 sq. ft.
Garage — 484 sq. ft.

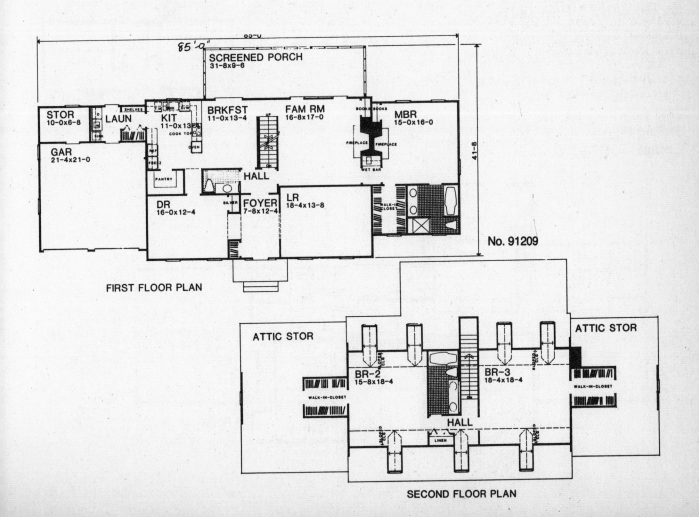

No. 91209

FIRST FLOOR PLAN

SECOND FLOOR PLAN

Unusual French Design

No. 90043

The glamour and serenity of French Provincial styling are on display throughout this unusual 1 1/2 story design. This is the perfect home for the family with a well developed feeling for traditional influence. Note the grand foyer with its circular staircase that flows up to the two second floor bedrooms; the sunken living room that is flanked with wrought iron rails and grilles; and the built-in wet bar and fireplace with French mantle in the family room. The master bedroom suite has two closets, a room-size walk-in, a dressing area vanity with full-length mirror, and a complete bath with double-basin vanity, sunken Roman tub, glass enclosed shower and sauna. Accessible to the rear sun-deck is the family room and the well equipped island kitchen.

First floor — 2,497 sq. ft.
Second floor — 527 sq. ft.
Garage — 550 sq. ft.

SECOND FLOOR PLAN

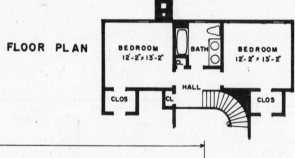

FIRST FLOOR PLAN

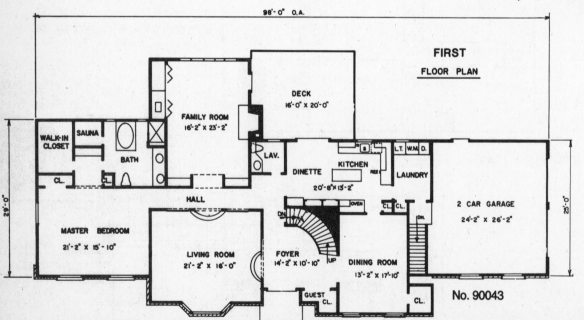

No. 90043

Wooden Decks are Nice for Summer Dining

No. 9308
Variegated brick, rich wood siding, and diamond light windows layer the exterior of this split foyer plan. Inside, four bedrooms and a den, plus a large recreation room provide space for privacy and relaxation. Besides the recreation room, a den, bedroom, utility and bath are found on the lower level. Upstairs, the comfortable living room enjoys a fireplace, and the dining room includes sliding glass doors to the elevated wooden deck.

Upper level — 1,440 sq. ft.
Lower level — 1,344 sq. ft.
Garage — 497 sq. ft.

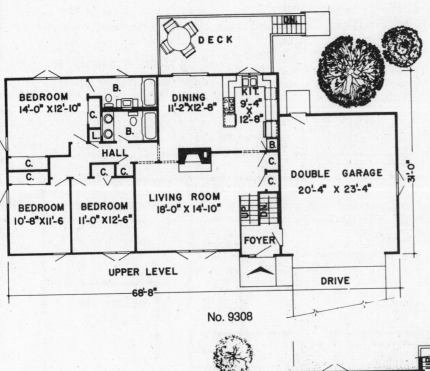

No. 9308

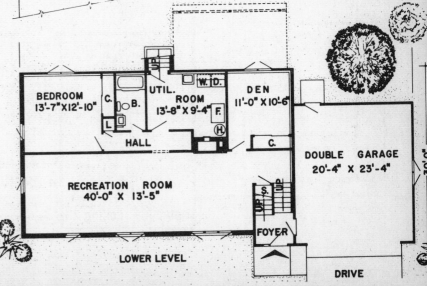

Compact Plan Allows For Gracious Living

No. 90158

A great room, accessible from the foyer, offers a cathedral ceiling with exposed beams, brick fireplace and access to the rear patio. The kitchen-breakfast area with center island and cathedral ceiling is accented by the round top window. The master bedroom has a full bath and walk-in closet. Two additional bedrooms and bath help make this an ideal plan for any growing family.

First floor—1,540 sq. ft.
Basement—1,540 sq. ft.

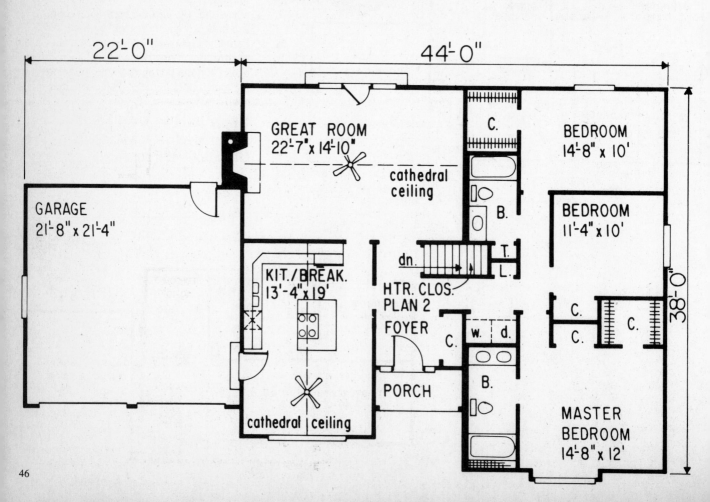

Generous Windows Flood Classic Home with Light

No. 10590

There are two ways to enter this charming saltbox: under the protected breezeway by the garage or through the formal central foyer. This traditional design has been updated to include a two-way fire-place between the living and family rooms, an open kitchen and breakfast nook, and a wooden deck accessible from the laundry or family rooms. The second floor houses four bedrooms and two baths.

First floor — 1,217 sq. ft.
Second floor — 1,154 sq. ft.
Basement — 1,217 sq. ft.
Garage — 581 sq. ft.
Breezeway — 210 sq. ft.

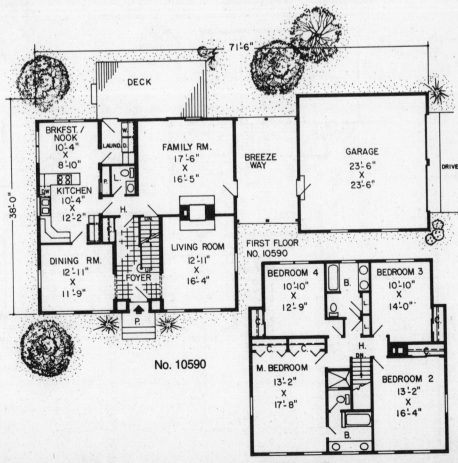

No. 10590

FIRST FLOOR
NO. 10590

SECOND FLOOR

Surround Yourself with Luxury

No. 10615

A magnificent home in every detail, this stately 5 bedroom residence surrounds you with thoughtful luxury. Enter the oversized, tiled foyer and view the grand staircase whose landing splits the ascent into separate wings and creates an aura of privacy for a guest or live-in relative in bedroom 4. Serenity reigns throughout the home thanks to the courtyard plan that insulates the master bedroom complex and bedroom 2 from the main living areas. The kitchen is designed to serve the eating areas and family room and reserve the vast living room for more formal entertaining. Most of the home shares access to, and wonderful views of, the patio, covered by the 2nd floor deck, and pool area.

First floor — 4,075 sq. ft.
Second floor — 1,179 sq. ft.
Garage — 633 sq. ft.

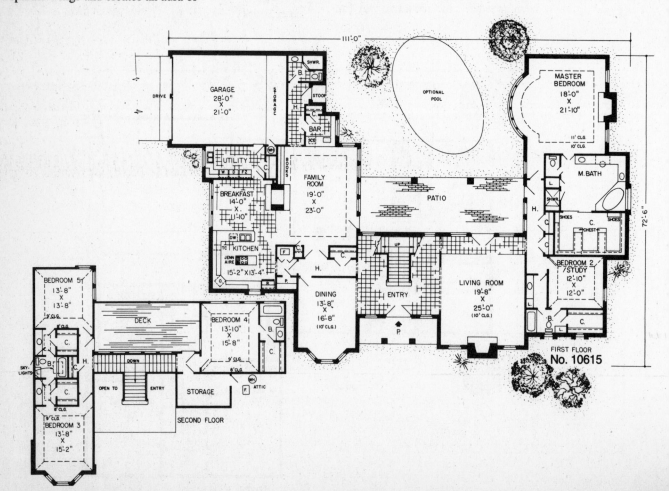

BEDROOM 12'-0"x17'-6"

DRESS

BATH

CLOSET

RAIL

SITTING 8'-0"x10'-8"

STORAGE 18'-0"x10'-4"

DN

STOR

BEDROOM 13'-0"x11'-10"

BEDROOM 12'-8"x11'-10"

CLOSET

CLOSET

DN

28'-6"

65'-6"

UPPER FLOOR PLAN

Bay Windows Enhance a Country Home

No. 90405

Large master bedroom suite includes deluxe bath with separate shower, garden tub, twin vanities and two large walk-in closets combine to form a super suite. Kitchen has direct access to both breakfast nook and dining room feature a large bay window. Three bedrooms, sitting area and storage or (bonus room) combine to form the second level.

First floor — 2,005 sq. ft.
Second floor — 1,063 sq. ft.

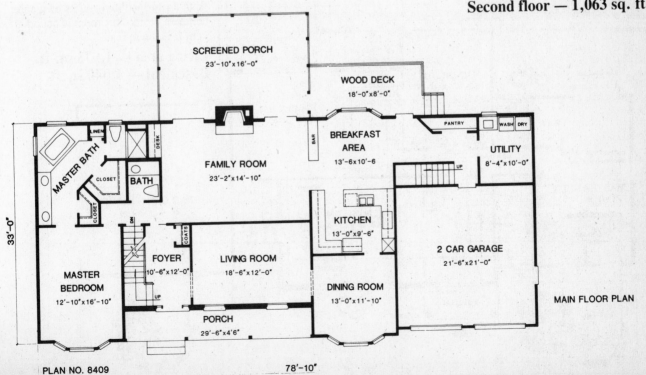

SCREENED PORCH 23'-10"x16'-0"

WOOD DECK 18'-0"x8'-0"

LINEN

MASTER BATH

CLOSET

BATH

DESK

FAMILY ROOM 23'-2"x14'-10"

BAR

BREAKFAST AREA 13'-6x10'-6

PANTRY

WASH DRY

UTILITY 8'-4"x10'-0"

UP

DN

COATS

FOYER 10'-6"x12'-0"

LIVING ROOM 18'-6"x12'-0"

KITCHEN 13'-0"x9'-6"

2 CAR GARAGE 21'-6"x21'-0"

UP

MASTER BEDROOM 12'-10"x16'-10"

DINING ROOM 13'-0"x11'-10"

PORCH 29'-6"x4'6"

33'-0"

PLAN NO. 8409

78'-10"

MAIN FLOOR PLAN

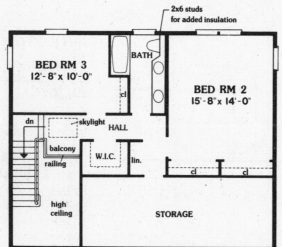

BED RM 3
12'-8" x 10'-0"

2x6 studs
for added insulation

BATH

BED RM 2
15'-8" x 14'-0"

cl

dn

skylight   HALL

balcony

railing

W.I.C.   lin.

cl   cl

high
ceiling

STORAGE

First Floor Master Suite is Special

No. 90624

American as apple pie, this three-bedroom Colonial classic has a welcoming warmth that will capture your fancy. The two-story foyer is lit from above by a skylight. Special features abound throughout the house: access the terrace or garage through the family room, a convenient kitchen which serves family and formal dining areas with ease, and a heatcirculating fireplace flanked by shelves in the living room. The spacious master suite, housed in a separate wing, has vaulted ceilings and is illuminated by spectacular windows on three walls. With a whirlpool tub and its own entertainment center, this room is bound to be your favorite retreat.

Living area — 1,973 sq. ft.
Basement — 1,340 sq. ft.

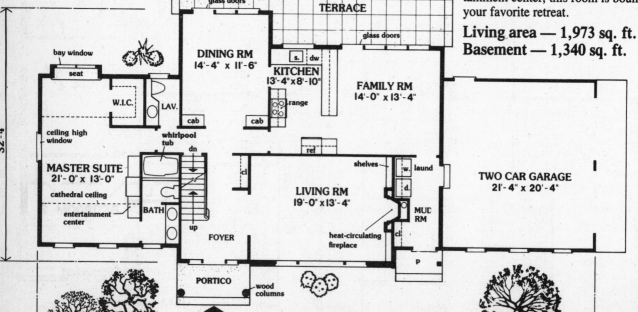

No. 90624

glass doors   TERRACE

glass doors

bay window

seat

W.I.C.   LAV.

DINING RM
14'-4" x 11'-6"

s.   dw

KITCHEN
13'-4" x 8'-10"

range

FAMILY RM
14'-0" x 13'-4"

ceiling high
window

cab   cab

whirlpool
tub

dn

ref

32'-4"

MASTER SUITE
21'-0" x 13'-0"

cathedral ceiling

entertainment
center

BATH

up

cl

shelves   w. laund

d.

LIVING RM
19'-0" x 13'-4"

TWO CAR GARAGE
21'-4" x 20'-4"

MUD
RM

FOYER

heat-circulating
fireplace

cl

p

PORTICO

wood
columns

75'-0"

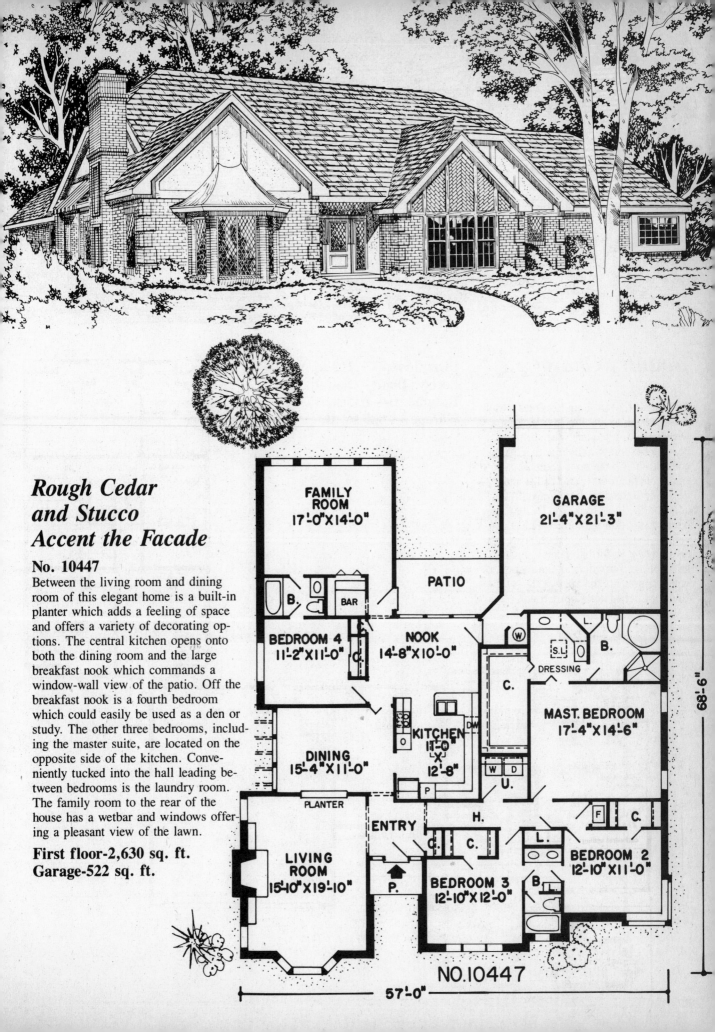

Rough Cedar and Stucco Accent the Facade

No. 10447

Between the living room and dining room of this elegant home is a built-in planter which adds a feeling of space and offers a variety of decorating options. The central kitchen opens onto both the dining room and the large breakfast nook which commands a window-wall view of the patio. Off the breakfast nook is a fourth bedroom which could easily be used as a den or study. The other three bedrooms, including the master suite, are located on the opposite side of the kitchen. Conveniently tucked into the hall leading between bedrooms is the laundry room. The family room to the rear of the house has a wetbar and windows offering a pleasant view of the lawn.

**First floor-2,630 sq. ft.
Garage-522 sq. ft.**

FAMILY ROOM 17'-0" X 14'-0"

GARAGE 21'-4" X 21'-3"

PATIO

B.

BAR

BEDROOM 4 11'-2" X 11'-0"

NOOK 14'-8" X 10'-0"

W

S.L.

DRESSING

B.

C.

MAST. BEDROOM 17'-4" X 14'-6"

KITCHEN 11'-0" X 12'-8"

DINING 15'-4" X 11'-0"

DW

W D

U.

PLANTER

P

F

C.

ENTRY

H.

LIVING ROOM 15'-10" X 19'-10"

P.

C.

C.

L.

BEDROOM 2 12'-10" X 11'-0"

BEDROOM 3 12'-10" X 12'-0"

B.

NO. 10447

68'-6"

57'-0"

Country Charm

No. 90936

This beautiful farmhouse updates a traditional design to modern lifestyles for a warm, inviting feeling. The sheltered porch leads into the foyer with a handy coat closet. Up the open staircase, you'll find three bedrooms, two baths, and a den. The stairs also divide main living areas on the first floor. The living room opens to the dining room, which is convenient to the kitchen, but set apart just enough to give formal meals a quiet atmosphere. For informal family hours, you'll appreciate the open design of the country kitchen and family room.

First floor — 1,212 sq. ft.
Second floor — 960 sq. ft.
Basement — 855 sq. ft.
Garage — 600 sq. ft.

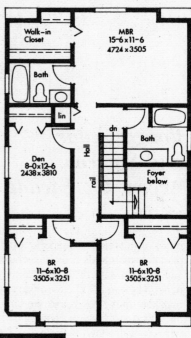

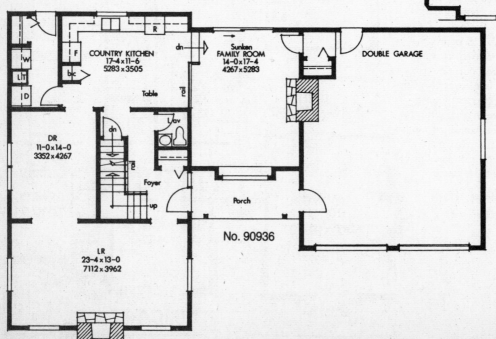

Home With A View

No. 10662

Here's a rambling classic that unites traditional elements with modern convenience. Columns adorn the entry and walled atrium. Stucco siding and a tile roof add to the classic beauty of the facade. With walls of windows in every room and french doors in the family room, you'll be able to enjoy your yard to its fullest advantage — even while you're inside. The huge cooktop island and central location make the kitchen a marvel of efficiency. And, you'll enjoy the first floor location of the master suite. Upstairs, double vanities in the full bath that adjoins the bedrooms make the morning rush easier.

First floor — 2,643 sq. ft.
Second floor — 927 sq. ft.
Garage — 1,170 sq. ft.

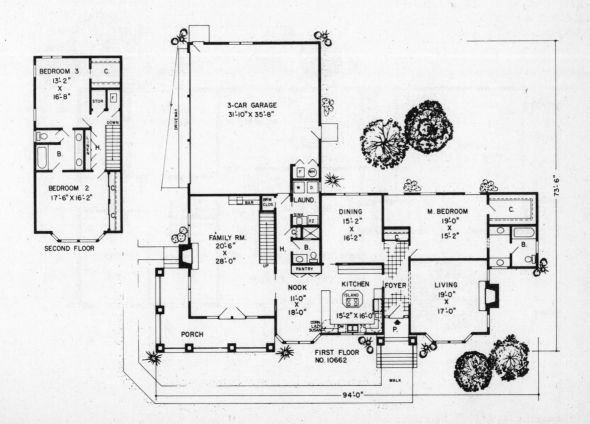

High Impact on a Low Budget

No. 10742

Build this Spanish-style, three bedroom gem on a slab to keep costs down and interest high. A trio of arches graces the porch of this one-level home, and provides a warm welcome to entering guests. Inside, dramatic cathedral ceilings bring an exciting atmosphere to the open living room, separated from the foyer by a half-wall, and warmed by a fireplace that dominates one wall. Soaring ceilings at the rear of the house are pierced by a skylight, bathing the dining room and island kitchen in warmth and light. The adjoining patio, accessible from the dining room and master suite, is a perfect spot to enjoy your first cup of coffee on a beautiful summer morning.

Main living area — 1,617 sq. ft.
Garage — 528 sq. ft.

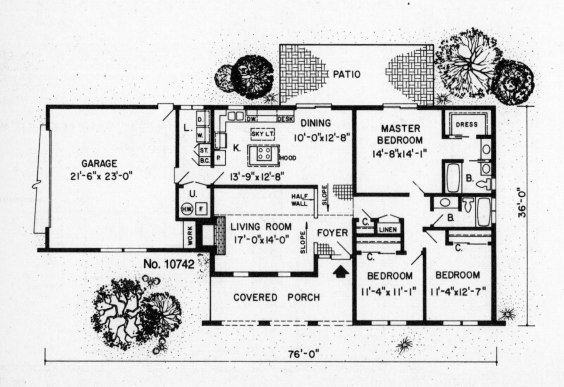

Dormers Provide
Cozy Window Seats

No. 90932

You'll find all the conveniences of modern living in this traditional New England Saltbox design. The attractive facade is authentic to the last detail, while inside the large foyer directs traffic with modern efficiency. The master suite on the main floor features his and hers closets. Close at hand is a large split-bath, which doubles as a powder room or guest bath. Mom will appreciate the lavatory next to the mud room at the rear door for youngsters returning from outdoor play. The stairs off the foyer lead up to two airy bedrooms featuring dramatic dormer window seats.

Main floor — 1,228 sq. ft.
Upper floor — 584 sq. ft.
Width — 52 ft.
Depth — 30 ft.

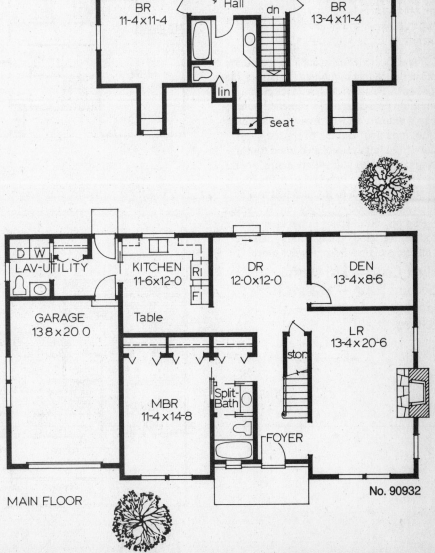

MAIN FLOOR

No. 90932

Compact Victorian Charmer

No. 91205

This home combines traditional and contemporary elements to achieve a modern masterpiece that combines the best of old and new. Features such as Victorian trim, multiple peaked roofs, a screened porch, bay windows, and an inviting porch hail from long ago. But the oversized windows, the huge, fireplaced great room, a country kitchen with sunny eating nook, and double sinks in both full baths upstairs are modern touches that make life easier for today's busy family. Notice the ample closet space in the three bedrooms, the handy garage entry, and the convenient, first-floor powder room.

**First floor — 888 sq. ft.
Second floor — 888 sq. ft.
Garage and storage — 336 sq. ft.**

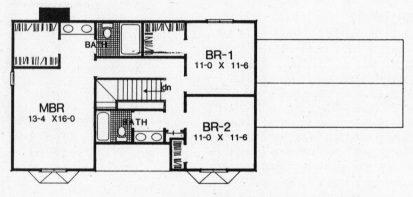

SECOND FLOOR

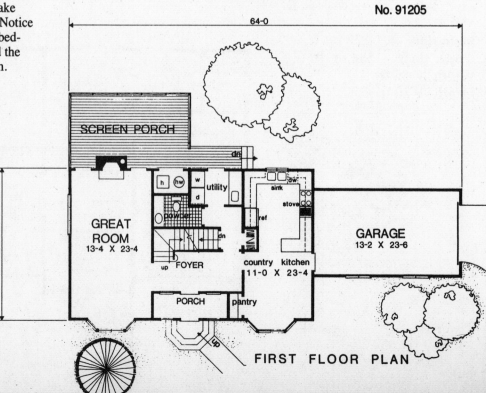

FIRST FLOOR PLAN

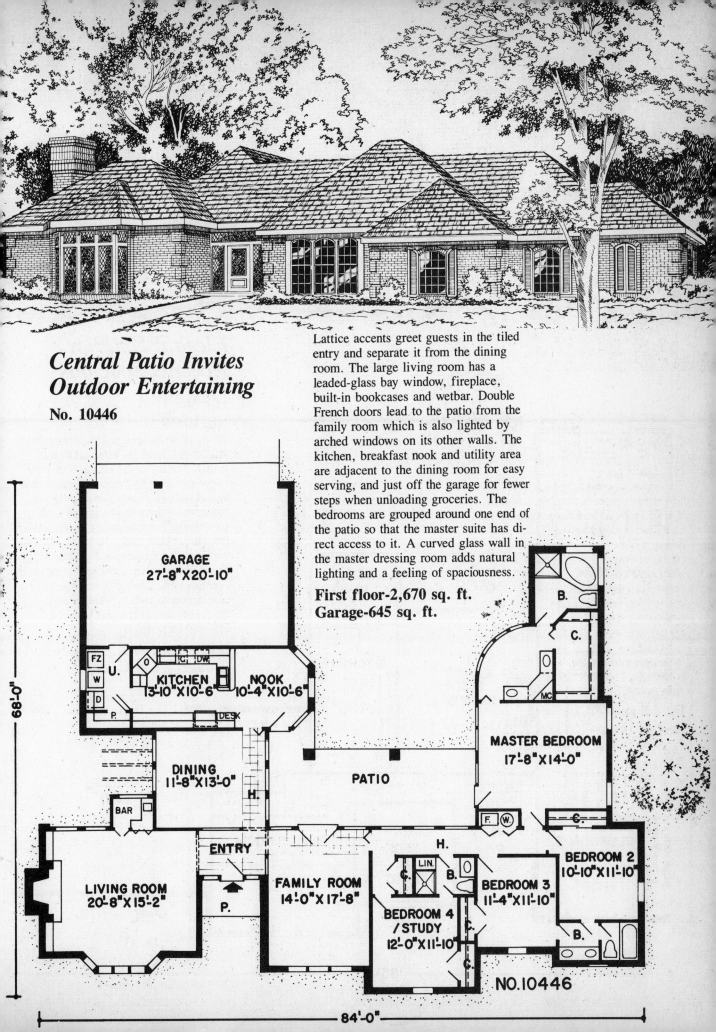

Central Patio Invites Outdoor Entertaining

No. 10446

Lattice accents greet guests in the tiled entry and separate it from the dining room. The large living room has a leaded-glass bay window, fireplace, built-in bookcases and wetbar. Double French doors lead to the patio from the family room which is also lighted by arched windows on its other walls. The kitchen, breakfast nook and utility area are adjacent to the dining room for easy serving, and just off the garage for fewer steps when unloading groceries. The bedrooms are grouped around one end of the patio so that the master suite has direct access to it. A curved glass wall in the master dressing room adds natural lighting and a feeling of spaciousness.

First floor-2,670 sq. ft.
Garage-645 sq. ft.

GARAGE
27'-8"X20'-10"

FZ U.
W
D
P.
KITCHEN
13'-10"X10'-6"
NOOK
10'-4"X10'-6"
DESK

DINING
11'-8"X13'-0"
H.

PATIO

MASTER BEDROOM
17'-8"X14'-0"

B.
C.
MC

BAR

ENTRY

P.

LIVING ROOM
20'-8"X15'-2"

FAMILY ROOM
14'-0"X17'-8"

H.

F. W.

C.

BEDROOM 2
10'-10"X11'-10"

LIN.
C.
B.

BEDROOM 3
11'-4"X11'-10"

BEDROOM 4 / STUDY
12'-0"X11'-10"

C.

B.

NO. 10446

68'-0"

84'-0"

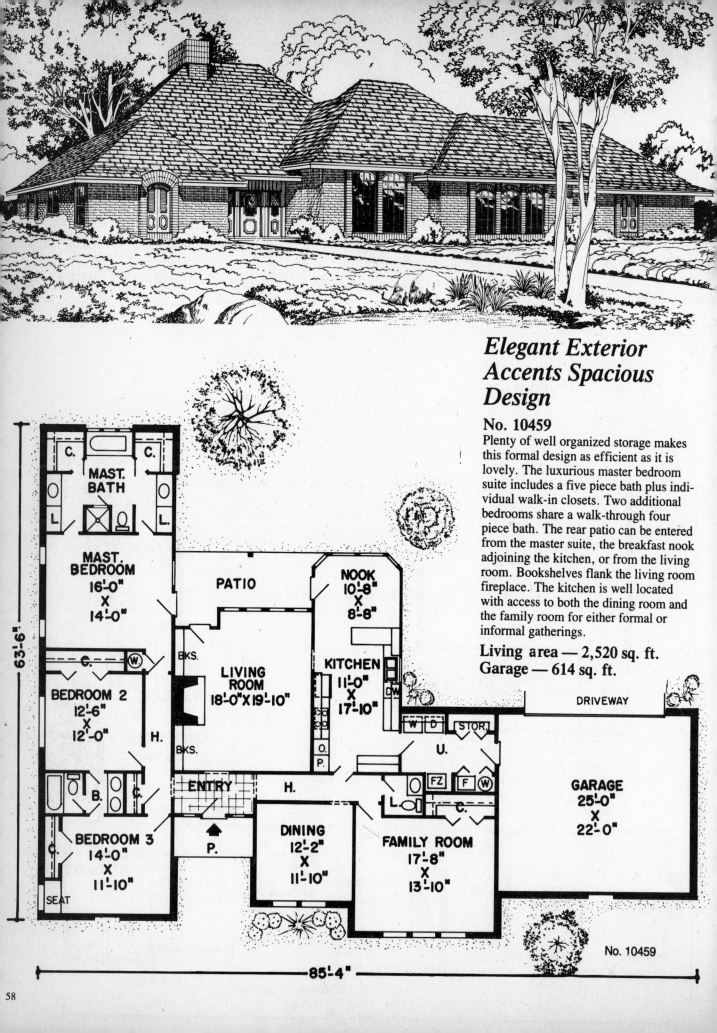

Elegant Exterior Accents Spacious Design

No. 10459

Plenty of well organized storage makes this formal design as efficient as it is lovely. The luxurious master bedroom suite includes a five piece bath plus individual walk-in closets. Two additional bedrooms share a walk-through four piece bath. The rear patio can be entered from the master suite, the breakfast nook adjoining the kitchen, or from the living room. Bookshelves flank the living room fireplace. The kitchen is well located with access to both the dining room and the family room for either formal or informal gatherings.

Living area — 2,520 sq. ft.
Garage — 614 sq. ft.

Luxurious Master Suite Lies Behind Double Doors

No. 90513

Two fireplaces warm this three bedroom abode with loads of outdoor living space. One covered porch shelters the entry. Another provides a perfect place to enjoy coffee off the dining room. And, a deck off the hallway upstairs and the breakfast nook below affords a golden opportunity for star gazing. Matching bay windows brighten the fireplaced living room and den. The sunny family room is just a step down from the island kitchen and breakfast nook.

First floor — 1,412 sq. ft.
Second floor — 1,080 sq. ft.

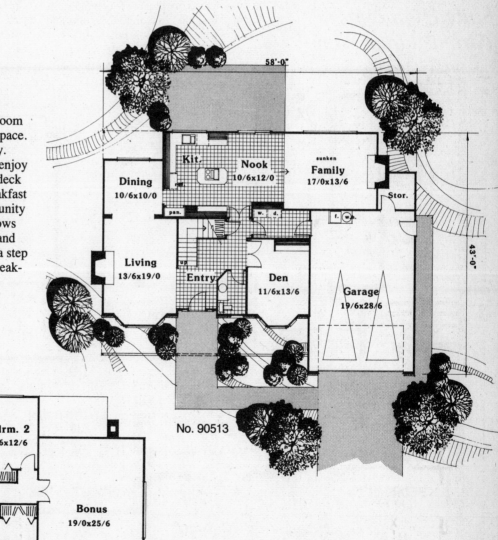

58'-0"

43'-0"

Kit.

Nook
10/6x12/0

sunken
Family
17/0x13/6

Dining
10/6x10/0

Stor.

pan.

w. d.

f. w.

Living
13/6x19/0

up

Entry

Den
11/6x13/6

Garage
19/6x28/6

No. 90513

Master
17/0x13/0

lin.

Bedrm. 2
11/6x12/6

dn

open to entry
below

Bonus
19/0x25/6

walk in
wardrobe

Bedrm. 3
10/0x16/0

tub

Upper Floor

Luxurious Master Suite Highlights Formal Floor Plan

No. 10451

Complete with its own private fireplace the master bedroom suite is complemented by individual dressing rooms and vanities plus the bathing area which is graced by a skylight. The covered patio also makes use of skylights and adds a sense of openness to both the family room and living room. Each of these rooms has a fireplace and they share a wetbar.

First floor — 2,864 sq. ft.
Garage — 607 sq. ft.

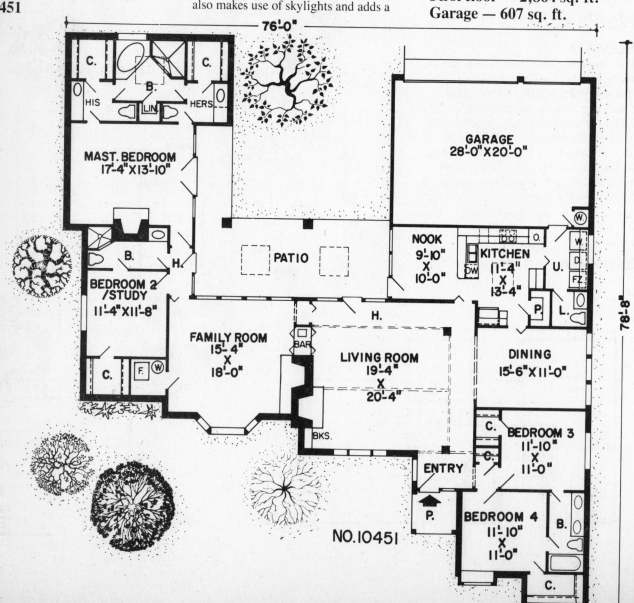

76'-0"

78'-8"

C.

B.

C.

HIS   LIN.   HERS

MAST. BEDROOM
17'-4" X 13'-10"

B.

H.

BEDROOM 2
/STUDY
11'-4" X 11'-8"

C.   F.   W.

FAMILY ROOM
15'-4"
X
18'-0"

BAR

BKS.

PATIO

GARAGE
28'-0" X 20'-0"

NOOK
9'-10"
X
10'-0"

KITCHEN
11'-4"
X
13'-4"

W.
O.
W
D
FZ
U.
P.
L.

H.

LIVING ROOM
19'-4"
X
20'-4"

DINING
15'-6" X 11'-0"

C.
C.

BEDROOM 3
11'-10"
X
11'-0"

ENTRY

P.

BEDROOM 4
11'-10"
X
11'-0"

B.

C.

NO. 10451

Entertaining is No Problem

No. 10610

Start picking out the porch furniture. You won't be able to resist sitting on this magnificent veranda on a lazy summer day. Walking through the front door, you'll encounter a large planter that divides the entry from active areas at the rear of the house. You'll find a sunny bay with built-in seating in the formal dining room, which shares a massive, two-way fireplace with the vaulted, sunken living room. If the living room bar doesn't fill all your entertaining needs, the nearby island kitchen certainly will. And, if the crowd gets too large, the full-length deck, accessible from the living room or breakfast room, can handle the overflow. There are two bedrooms and a full bath on the first floor, but the master suite enjoys a private location at the top of the stairs.

First floor — 1,818 sq. ft.
Second floor — 528 sq. ft.
Basement — 1,818 sq. ft.

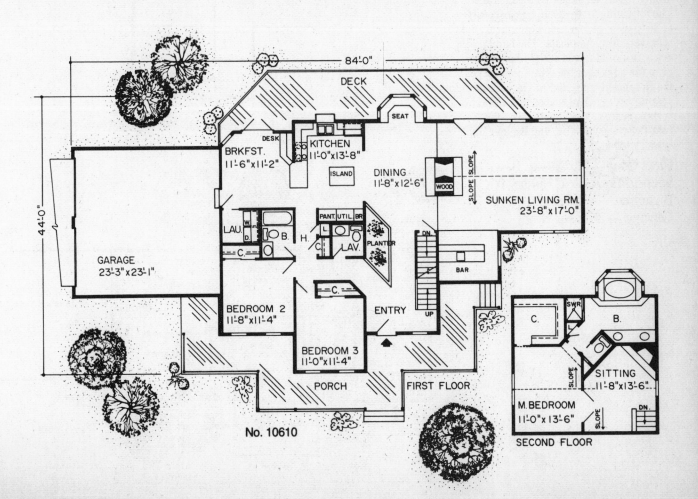

No. 10610

Elegant and Inviting

No. 10689

Traditional and modern elements unite to create an outstanding plan for the family that enjoys outdoor entertaining. Wrap-around verandas and a three-season porch insure the party will stay dry, rain or shine. You may want to keep guests inside, in the elegant parlor and formal dining room, separated by a half wall. The adjoining kitchen can be closed off to keep meal preparation convenient, but removed from the bustle. The family will enjoy informal meals at the island bar, or in the adjoining breakfast nook. Even the fireplaced gathering room, with its soaring ceilings and access to the porch, is right nearby. You'll appreciate the first-floor master suite, and the upstairs laundry location.

First floor — 1,580 sq. ft.
Second floor — 1,164 sq. ft.
Basement — 1,329 sq. ft.
Garage — 576 sq. ft.

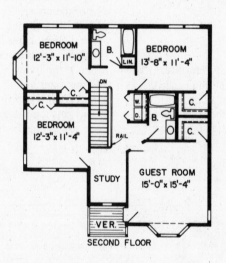

A Design by William E. Gage

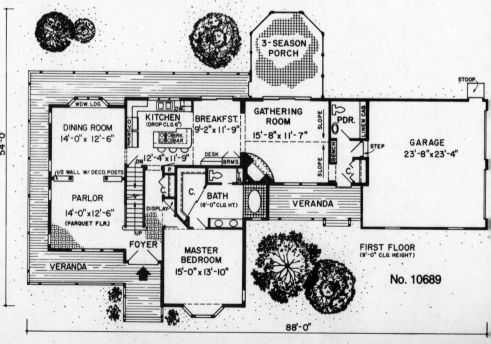

Attractive Floor Plan Enhances Traditional Design

No. 20056

This three-bedroom, two-bath home offers comfort and style. The master bedroom is complete with its own bath with a skylight. A beamed ceiling and fireplace in the living area add charm to the more traditional family room. A spacious laundry room adjoins the kitchen and breakfast area. The country-style front porch and large front windows in the breakfast and dining rooms lend a cozy atmosphere to this eye-catching design.

First floor — 1,669 sq. ft.
Basement — 1,669 sq. ft.
Garage — 482 sq. ft.

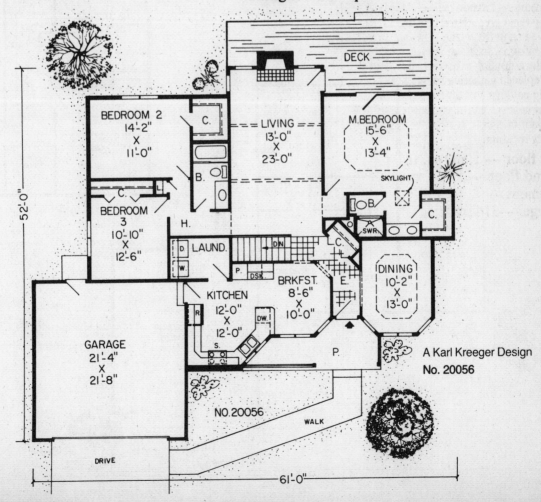

A Karl Kreeger Design
No. 20056

Rooms of their Own

No. 10592

If you want a traditional house with lots of room for growth, you'll love this 4 bedroom, 2 1/2 bath saltbox with attached two car garage. Access all the rooms on the first floor from the central foyer. Sharing a double fireplace with the living room, the family room features sliding glass doors to the deck outside. You'll find ample closets in every bedroom upstairs. And, the double sink is handy for those hectic mornings when the school bus is on its way.

First floor — 1,318 sq. ft.
Second floor — 1,267 sq. ft.
Basement — 559 sq. ft.
Garage — 1,225 sq. ft.

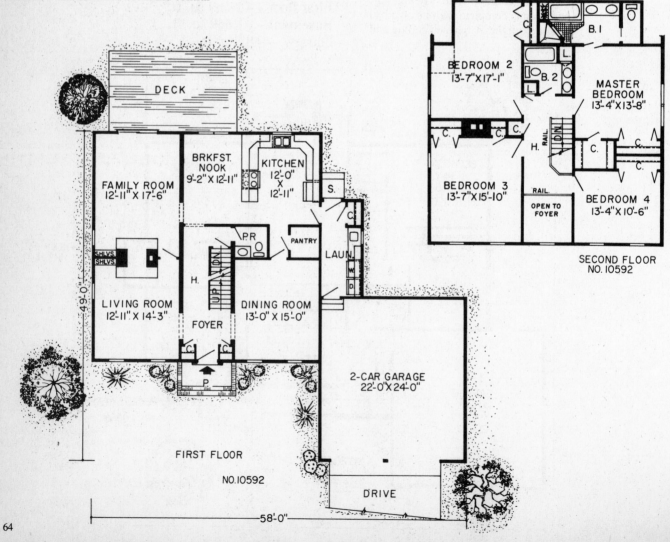

DECK

FAMILY ROOM
12'-11" X 17'-6"

BRKFST. NOOK
9'-2" X 12'-11"

KITCHEN
12'-0" X 12'-11"

S.

P.R

PANTRY

LAUN.

SHLVS

LIVING ROOM
12'-11" X 14'-3"

H.

FOYER

DINING ROOM
13'-0" X 15'-0"

C

P

49'-0"

2-CAR GARAGE
22'-0" X 24'-0"

FIRST FLOOR
NO. 10592

DRIVE

58'-0"

BEDROOM 2
13'-7" X 17'-1"

B.1

B.2

L

C

MASTER BEDROOM
13'-4" X 13'-8"

BEDROOM 3
13'-7" X 15'-10"

C.

H.

RAIL.

DN

OPEN TO FOYER

RAIL.

BEDROOM 4
13'-4" X 10'-6"

C.

SECOND FLOOR
NO. 10592

Wrought Iron Courtyard Adds to Design

No. 10562

This brick front ranch uses horizontal siding on its side and back exterior walls.

Inside, three bedroons are offered, in which two share a full and a half-bath. The master bedroom has its own full bath area. The living room has a display shelf built in and its own wood-burning fireplace. The kitchen has both a meal preparation island and its own breakfast nook and is designed with no partitions, providing more open space for furniture arrangements. A closet pantry is located within the kitchen, eliminating unnecessary steps for meal preparation. The dining room is made more formal with a vaulted ceiling design. A two-car garage is offered in this plan.

Living Area — 2,155 sq. ft.
Basement — 2,155 sq. ft.
Garage — 586 sq. ft.

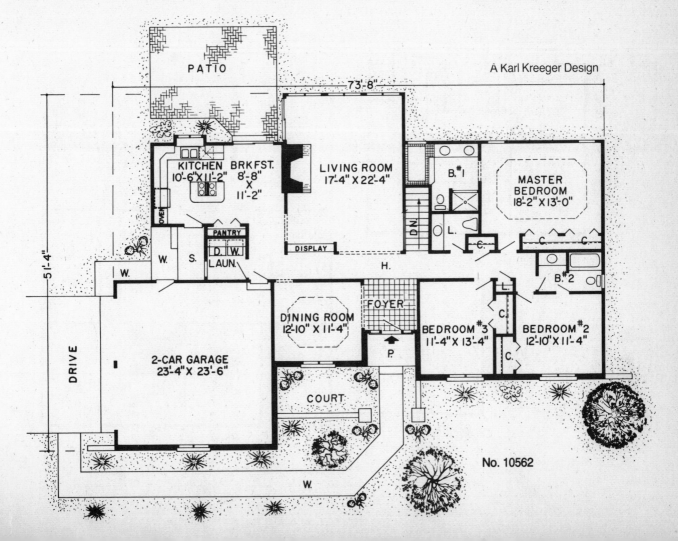

A Karl Kreeger Design

No. 10562

Colonial Warmth

No. 10580

Expansive rooms distinguish this gracious dwelling with both central and sheltered kitchen entries. The foyer leads to the dining room and parlor, each warmed by a cozy fireplace. The rustic gathering room and kitchen are like one huge room, separated only by an ample work island with double ovens. Walk out to the deck and screened gazebo from the gathering room or rear hall doorway adjacent to laundry and powder room. Two separate stairways provide access to the fireplaced master suite, two additional bedrooms, and two full baths.

First floor — 1,769 sq. ft.
Second floor — 1,156 sq. ft.
Basement — 1,769 sq. ft.
Garage — 667 sq. ft.

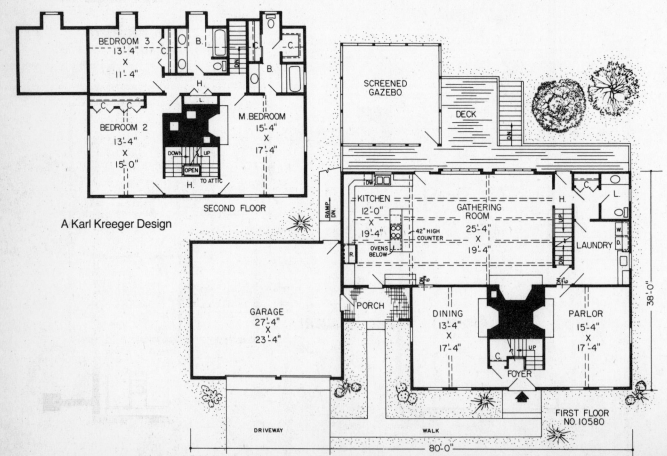

A Karl Kreeger Design

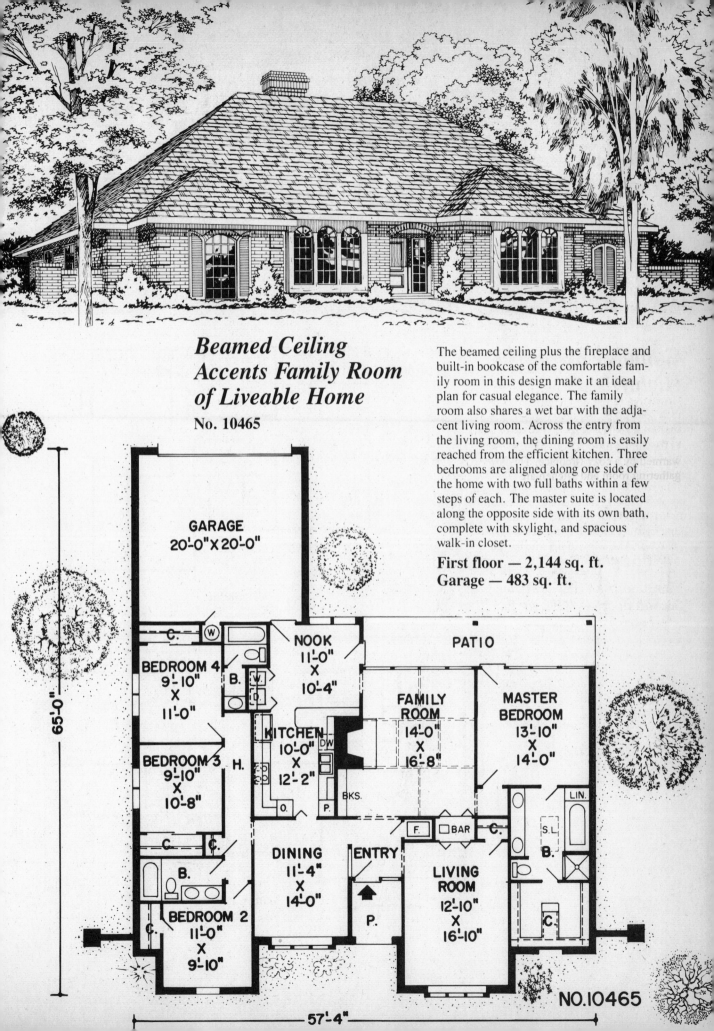

Beamed Ceiling Accents Family Room of Liveable Home

No. 10465

The beamed ceiling plus the fireplace and built-in bookcase of the comfortable family room in this design make it an ideal plan for casual elegance. The family room also shares a wet bar with the adjacent living room. Across the entry from the living room, the dining room is easily reached from the efficient kitchen. Three bedrooms are aligned along one side of the home with two full baths within a few steps of each. The master suite is located along the opposite side with its own bath, complete with skylight, and spacious walk-in closet.

First floor — 2,144 sq. ft.
Garage — 483 sq. ft.

GARAGE
20'-0" X 20'-0"

BEDROOM 4
9'-10"
X
11'-0"

BEDROOM 3
9'-10"
X
10'-8"

NOOK
11'-0"
X
10'-4"

PATIO

FAMILY ROOM
14'-0"
X
16'-8"

MASTER BEDROOM
13'-10"
X
14'-0"

KITCHEN
10'-0"
X
12'-2"

BKS.

LIN.

S.L.

DINING
11'-4"
X
14'-0"

ENTRY

LIVING ROOM
12'-10"
X
16'-10"

BEDROOM 2
11'-0"
X
9'-10"

F. BAR

65'-0"

57'-4"

NO. 10465

Windows are Highlights

No. 90118

Double windows in the living room and formal dining room, plus a bay window off the kitchen's dining area, enhance the livability of this spacious home. With your choice of four or five bedrooms, all located upstairs for privacy, individuality flourishes. There's even a mud room conveniently located to the rear of the garage and adjacent to the kitchen for cleaning up after yard work.

First floor — 1,392 sq. ft.
Second floor — 1,282 sq. ft.

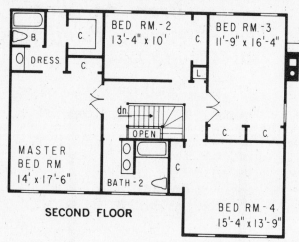

SECOND FLOOR

No. 90118

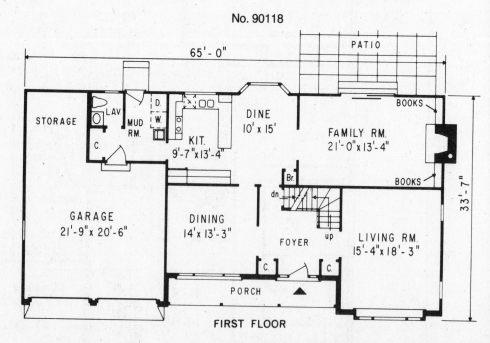

FIRST FLOOR

Fireplace Inspires Romantic Dining

No. 9908

Pleasurable dining in the expansive living-dining area is created by the atmospheric wood-burning fireplace in this brick-layered traditional. A functional breakfast bar joins the kitchen and family room, which is placed to enjoy the terrace. A gracious foyer eliminates cross-traffic and allows access to the living or sleeping wing, where three sizable bedrooms and two full baths are provided. The double garage also opens to the terrace.

Main floor — 1,896 sq. ft.
Basement — 1,896 sq. ft.
Garage — 509 sq. ft.

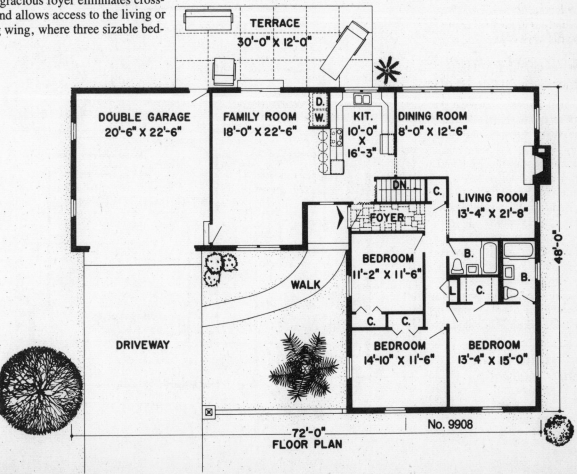

No. 9908
FLOOR PLAN

SECOND FLOOR

BEDROOM
13'-6" X 13'-4"

SLOPED CEILING

WALK-IN CLOSET

HALL

BATH

LINEN

STORAGE

OPEN

RAIL

DOWN

LINEN

WALK-IN CLOSET

BEDROOM
12'-4" X 15'-4"

Basement with Drive-Under Garage

No. 90401

This rustic design includes a two-car garage as part of its full basement. All or part of the basement can be used to supplement the main living area. The master suite features a large walk-in closet and a double vanity in the master bath. An L-shaped kitchen with dining bay, a living room with raised-hearth fireplace and a centrally located utility room complete the main floor. The open two-story foyer leads to the upper floor consisting of two bedrooms with walk-in closets and a second full bath with two linen closets. Front porch, multi-paned windows, shutters and horizontal wood siding combine for a rustic exterior. Basement foundation only.

First floor — 1,100 sq. ft.
Second floor — 660 sq. ft.

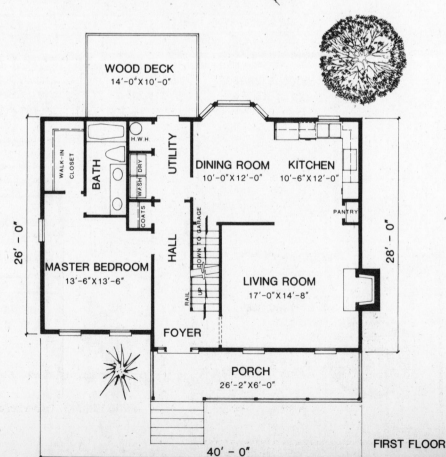

WOOD DECK
14'-0" X 10'-0"

WALK-IN CLOSET

BATH

H.W.H.

WASH DRY

COATS

UTILITY

DINING ROOM
10'-0" X 12'-0"

KITCHEN
10'-6" X 12'-0"

PANTRY

HALL

DOWN TO GARAGE

UP

RAIL

MASTER BEDROOM
13'-6" X 13'-6"

LIVING ROOM
17'-0" X 14'-8"

FOYER

26'-0"

28'-0"

PORCH
26'-2" X 6'-0"

40'-0"

FIRST FLOOR

Music Room Enhances Special Design

No. 10584

If music is the love of your life, consider this special home. A remarkable chamber with cathedral ceiling and built-in cabinets is devoted to the pleasures of sound. The rest of the home is stylish as well.

The handsome kitchen serves an eating bar as well as a breakfast room and large dining area with vaulted ceiling. The master bedroom enjoys a bath with walk-in closet. Large bedrooms inhabit the 2nd floor with a loft area that overlooks the foyer below. Gracious touches like the breezeway, screened porch, and courtyards complete a magnificent home.

First floor — 1,860 sq. ft.
Second floor — 901 sq. ft.
Basement — 1,823 sq. ft.
Screened porch — 168 sq. ft.
Breezeway — 112 sq. ft.
Garage — 677 sq. ft.

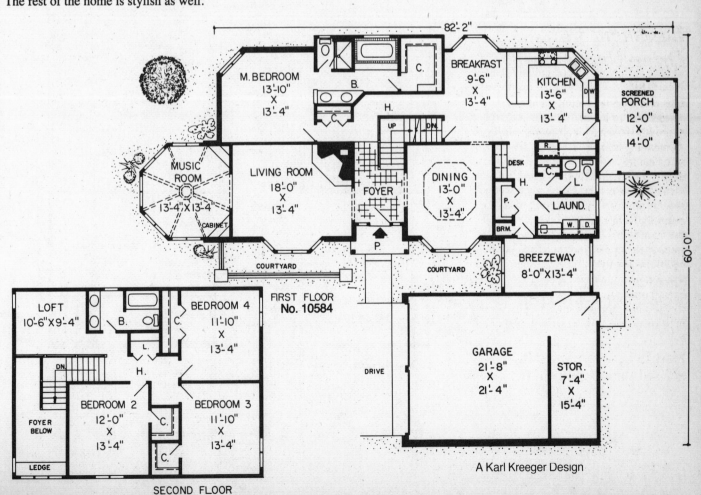

A Karl Kreeger Design

Old Fashion Charm

No. 21124

An old fashioned, homespun flavor has been created by using lattice work, horizontal and vertical placement of wood siding, and full length front and rear porches with turned wood columns and wood railings. The floor plan features an open living room, dining room and kitchen. A master suite finishes the first level. An additional bedroom and full bath are located upstairs. Here also is found a large bonus room which could serve a variety of family needs. Or it can be deleted altogether by adding a second balcony overlooking the living room below and allowing the living room ceilings to rise two full stories. Wood floors throughout the design add a final bit of country to the plan.

First floor — 835 sq. ft.
Second floor — 817 sq. ft.

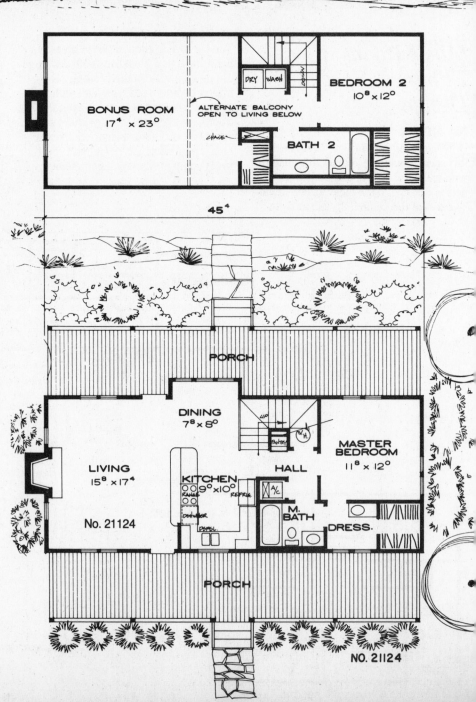

BONUS ROOM
17⁴ × 23⁰

ALTERNATE BALCONY
OPEN TO LIVING BELOW

DRY WASH

BEDROOM 2
10⁸ × 12⁰

BATH 2

CHASE

45⁴

PORCH

DINING
7⁸ × 8⁰

UP

MASTER BEDROOM
11⁸ × 12⁰

LIVING
15⁸ × 17⁴

KITCHEN
9⁰ × 10⁰

HALL

M. BATH

DRESS.

RANGE

REFRIG.

A/C

PANTRY

DISHWASHER

DISPOSAL

No. 21124

PORCH

NO. 21124

Brick-layered Home Plans 4 Bedrooms

No. 22004

Four roomy bedrooms, featuring a master bedroom with extra large bath, equip this plan for a large family or overnight guests. The centrally located family room merits a fireplace, wet bar, and access to the patio, and a dining room is provided for formal entertaining. An interesting kitchen and nook, as well as two and one half baths, are featured.

House-2,070 sq. ft.
Garage-474 sq. ft.

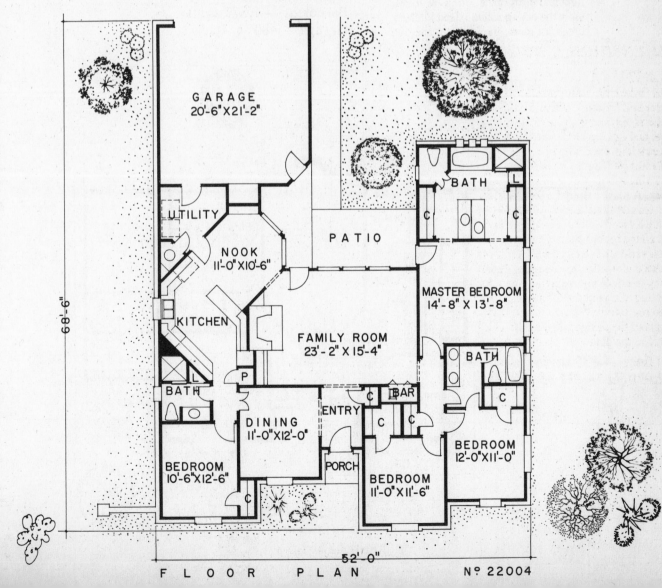

GARAGE
20'-6" X 21'-2"

UTILITY

NOOK
11'-0" X 10'-6"

PATIO

KITCHEN

BATH

MASTER BEDROOM
14'-8" X 13'-8"

FAMILY ROOM
23'-2" X 15'-4"

BATH

BATH

P

ENTRY

BAR

DINING
11'-0" X 12'-0"

BEDROOM
10'-6" X 12'-6"

PORCH

BEDROOM
11'-0" X 11'-6"

BEDROOM
12'-0" X 11'-0"

68'-6"

52'-0"

FLOOR PLAN   Nº 22004

Railing Divides Living Spaces

No. 10596

This one-level design is a celebration of light and open space. From the foyer, view the dining room, island kitchen, breakfast room, living room, and outdoor deck in one sweeping glance. Bay windows add pleasing angles and lots of sunshine to eating areas and the master suite. And, a wall of windows brings the outdoors into the two back bedrooms.

Upper floor — 1,740 sq. ft.
Basement — 1,377 sq. ft.
Garage — 480 sq. ft.

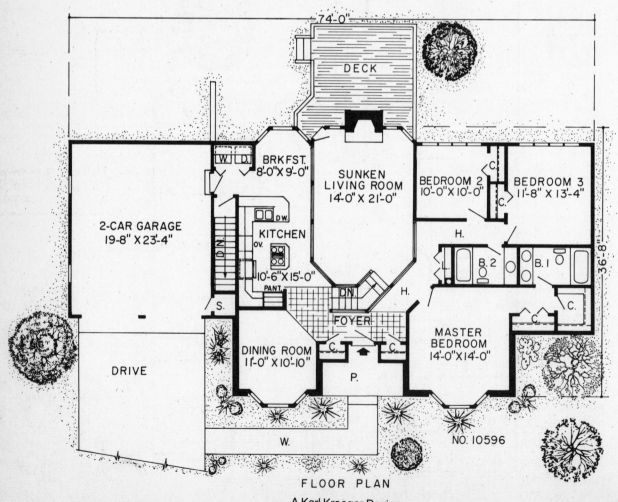

FLOOR PLAN

A Karl Kreeger Design

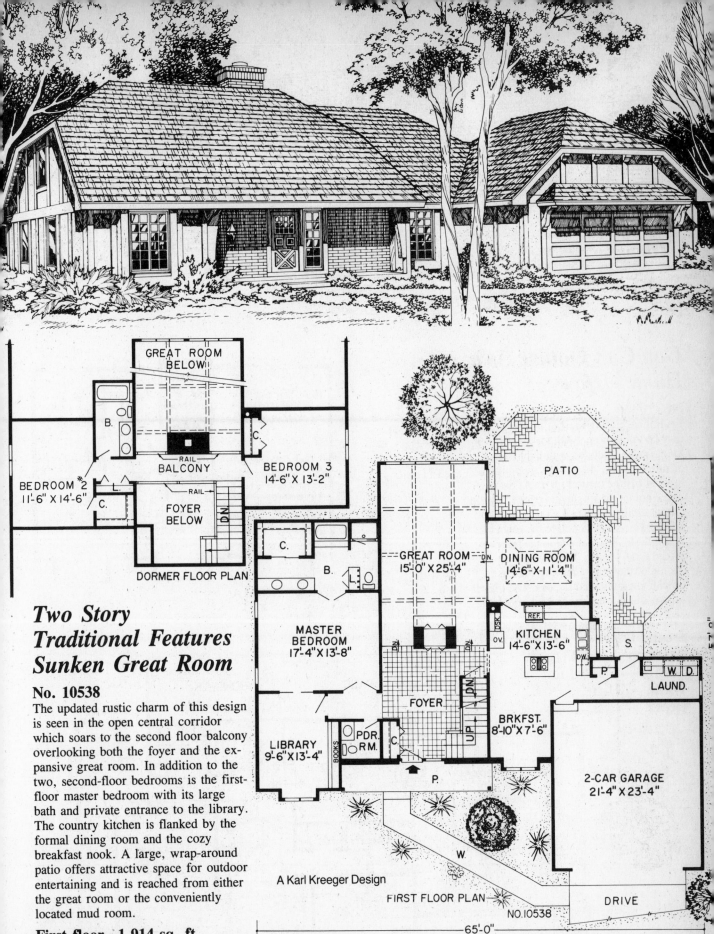

Two Story Traditional Features Sunken Great Room

No. 10538

The updated rustic charm of this design is seen in the open central corridor which soars to the second floor balcony overlooking both the foyer and the expansive great room. In addition to the two, second-floor bedrooms is the first-floor master bedroom with its large bath and private entrance to the library. The country kitchen is flanked by the formal dining room and the cozy breakfast nook. A large, wrap-around patio offers attractive space for outdoor entertaining and is reached from either the great room or the conveniently located mud room.

First floor—1,914 sq. ft.
Second floor—584 sq. ft.
Basement—1,900 sq. ft.
Garage—519 sq. ft.

GREAT ROOM BELOW

B.

RAIL
BALCONY

C.

BEDROOM 3
14'-6" X 13'-2"

BEDROOM #2
11'-6" X 14'-6"

L.

C.

RAIL

FOYER BELOW

DN

DORMER FLOOR PLAN

PATIO

C.

B.

L.

GREAT ROOM
15'-0" X 25'-4"

DN

DINING ROOM
14'-6" X 11'-4"

REF.

KITCHEN
14'-6" X 13'-6"

DSK

OV.

DW.

S.

MASTER BEDROOM
17'-4" X 13'-8"

DN

FOYER

DN

UP

P.

W. D.

LAUND.

BRKFST.
8'-10" X 7'-6"

LIBRARY
9'-6" X 13'-4"

BOOKS

PDR. RM.

C.

P.

2-CAR GARAGE
21'-4" X 23'-4"

W.

A Karl Kreeger Design

FIRST FLOOR PLAN
NO.10538

DRIVE

65'-0"

Den Can Double As a Home Office

No. 90816

Traditional styling marks this elegant, four-bedroom home with lots of outdoor living space. Flooded with light from a picture window, the sunken living room lies just off the central foyer. At the rear of the home, the kitchen is flanked by the formal dining room and a breakfast nook. Sliding glass doors open to the sundeck. A single step leads down to the fire-placed family room. Window gables at the top of the gently curving staircase provide pleasing study nooks. The master suite features a luxurious whirlpool bath.

First floor — 1,252 sq. ft.
Second floor — 1,117 sq. ft.
Basement — 1,246 sq. ft.
Garage — 564 sq. ft.
Width — 71 ft.
Depth — 35 ft.

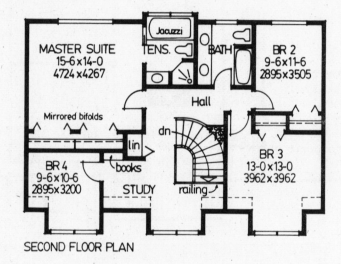

SECOND FLOOR PLAN

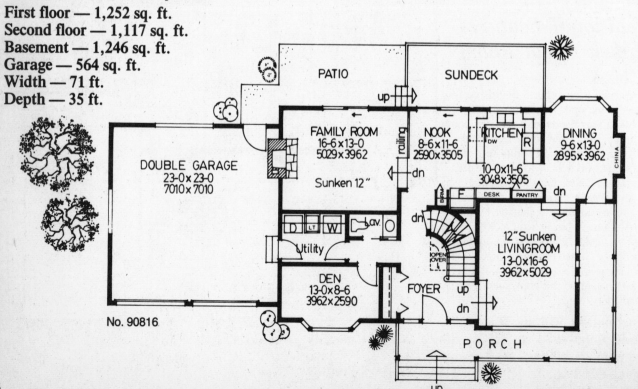

No. 90816

Traditional Energy-Saver

No. 20071

Take advantage of a southern exposure and save on energy costs in this beautiful family tudor. Heat is stored in the floor of the sun room, adjoining the living and breakfast rooms. When the sun goes down, close the french doors and light a fire in the massive fireplace. State-of-the-

art energy saving is not the only modern convenience in this house. You'll love the balcony overlooking the soaring two-story foyer and living room. In addition to providing great views, the balcony links the upstairs bedrooms. You're sure to enjoy the island kitchen, centrally located between formal and informal dining rooms. And, you'll never want to leave the luxurious master suite, with its double vanities and step-up whirlpool.

First floor — 2,186 sq. ft.
Second floor — 983 sq. ft.
Basement — 2,186 sq. ft.
Garage — 704 sq. ft.

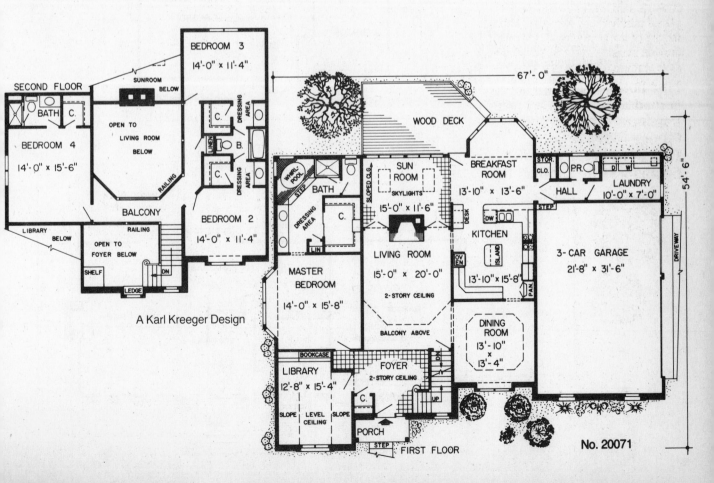

A Karl Kreeger Design

No. 20071

Classic and Comfortable

No. 90435

A central staircase dominates the spacious foyer of this efficient Tudor home. The convenient, L-shaped arrangement of kitchen, formal, and informal dining rooms means meal service will be a breeze. And, the elegance of a massive fireplace, french doors, and an adjoining rear deck make the great room a special spot. With three bedrooms and two full baths, there's room for the whole family upstairs. Use the bayed study off the master suite as a nursery, or a quiet getaway for those rare moments when you have time to relax.

First floor — 1,032 sq. ft.
Second floor — 1,050 sq. ft.

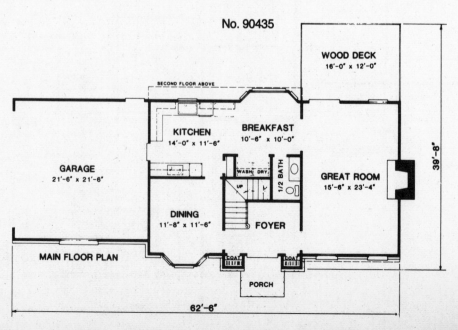

Porch Fronts
Charming Traditional

No. 19769

Extending across the front of this two story home, a porch adds interest as well as protection from wind and weather. The livable floor plan calls for a main level powder room, a combination hobby room and laundry, an open kitchen-dining area, and a spacious bedroom. Upstairs, two bedrooms share a full bath and merit plenty of closets and storage space.

First floor — 1,140 sq. ft.
Second floor — 607 sq. ft.
Basement — 1,140 sq. ft.
Garage — 675 sq. ft.

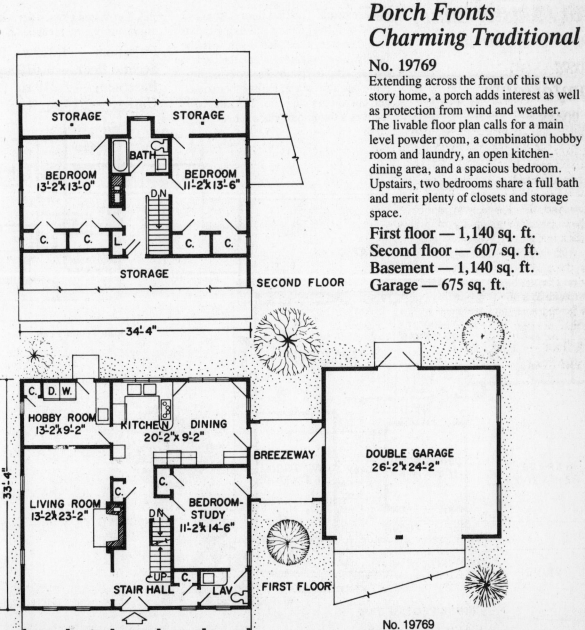

STORAGE   STORAGE

BATH

BEDROOM
13'-2"x13'-0"

BEDROOM
11'-2"x13'-6"

DN

C.   C.   L   C.   C.

STORAGE

SECOND FLOOR

34'-4"

C. D. W.

HOBBY ROOM
13'-2"x9'-2"

KITCHEN   DINING
20'-2"x9'-2"

BREEZEWAY

DOUBLE GARAGE
26'-2"x24'-2"

C.

LIVING ROOM
13'-2"x23'-2"

DN

BEDROOM-
STUDY
11'-2"x14'-6"

UP   C.

33'-4"

STAIR HALL   LAV

FIRST FLOOR

72'-2"

No. 19769

Luxury Master Suite, Room to Expand

No. 10525

In addition to three bedrooms, the second floor of this traditional design features a large unfinished area. The luxury master suite has two walk-in closets in the dressing area plus a five-piece bath which features a circular window above the tiled tub enclosure. The first floor is composed of formal dining and living rooms on either side of the tiled foyer, with the family areas organized along the back overlooking the patio. The cozy family room has a fireplace, built-in bookcase and opens onto the patio. The kitchen features a bump-out window over the sink and shares a snack bar with the bright and cheery breakfast nook.

First floor — 1,219 sq. ft.
Second floor — 1,010 sq. ft.
Basement — 1,219 sq. ft.
Garage — 514 sq. ft.

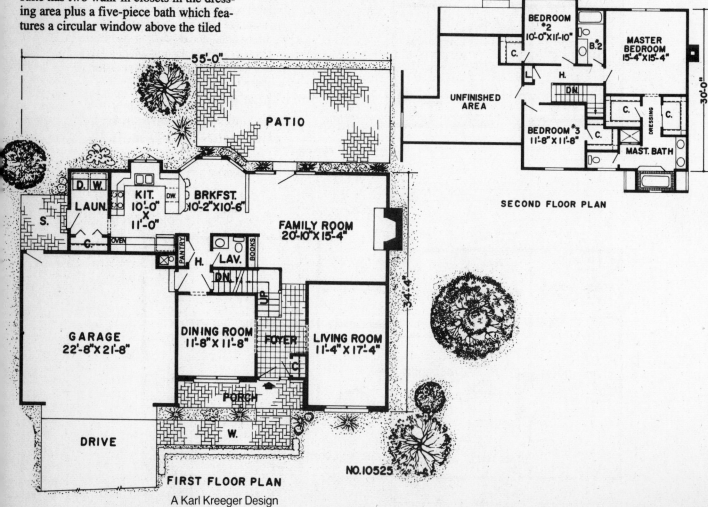

SECOND FLOOR PLAN

FIRST FLOOR PLAN

NO. 10525

A Karl Kreeger Design

Compact Victorian Ideal for Narrow Lot

No. 90406

This compact Victorian design incorporates four bedrooms and three full baths into a 30 foot wide home. The upstairs master suite features two closets, an oversized tub, and a sitting room with vaulted ceiling and bay window. Two additional bedrooms and a second full bath are included in the upper level. A fourth bedroom and third full bath on the main floor can serve as an in-law or guest suite. Between the dining and breakfast rooms is a galley kitchen. The dining room has a bay window and the breakfast room a utility nook. A large parlor with a raised-hearth fireplace completes the main floor. The porches add to the overall exterior appearances and help to protect the front and side entrances.

First floor — 954 sq. ft.
Second floor — 783 sq. ft.

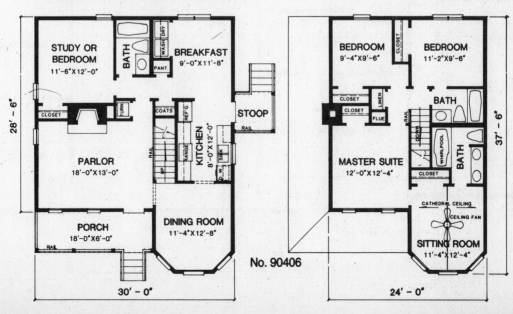

No. 90406

Fireplace Dominates Rustic Design

No. 90409

The ample porch of this charming home deserves a rocking chair, and there's room for two or three if you'd like. The front entry opens to an expansive great room with a soaring cathedral ceiling.

Flanked by the master suite and two bedrooms with a full bath, the great room is separated from formal dining by a massive fireplace. The convenient galley kitchen adjoins a sunny breakfast nook, perfect for informal family dining.

Living area — 1,670 sq. ft.

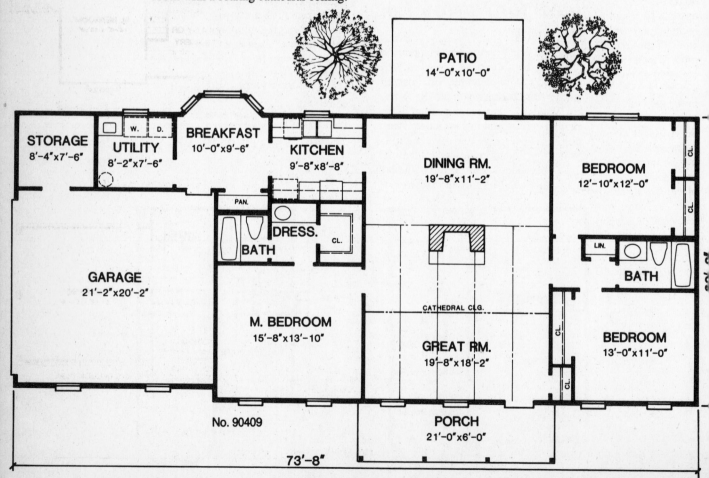

STORAGE
8'-4"x7'-6"

UTILITY
8'-2"x7'-6"

BREAKFAST
10'-0"x9'-6"

KITCHEN
9'-8"x8'-8"

PATIO
14'-0"x10'-0"

DINING RM.
19'-8"x11'-2"

BEDROOM
12'-10"x12'-0"

PAN.

DRESS.

BATH

CL.

LIN.

BATH

GARAGE
21'-2"x20'-2"

M. BEDROOM
15'-8"x13'-10"

CATHEDRAL CLG.

CL.

GREAT RM.
19'-8"x18'-2"

CL.

BEDROOM
13'-0"x11'-0"

No. 90409

PORCH
21'-0"x6'-0"

73'-8"

Room for Growth

No. 90434

Solid and dignified, this Tudor classic with attached two-car garage is a perfect home for your growing family. Three upstairs bedrooms and two full baths include a master suite with adjoining study or nursery. But, this house is a great place to entertain, too. A welcoming entry, convenient coat closets, and a handy first-floor powder room will make your guests feel at home immediately, and simplify your job as host. Serve dinner in the elegant formal dining room, an easy task with the convenience of an adjoining kitchen. The massive great room, dominated by a stone fireplace, can accommodate a crowd of any size. And, on a warm summer night, the rear deck or covered portico of the great room are perfect for star-gazing.

First floor — 1,252 sq. ft.
Second floor — 1,244 sq. ft.

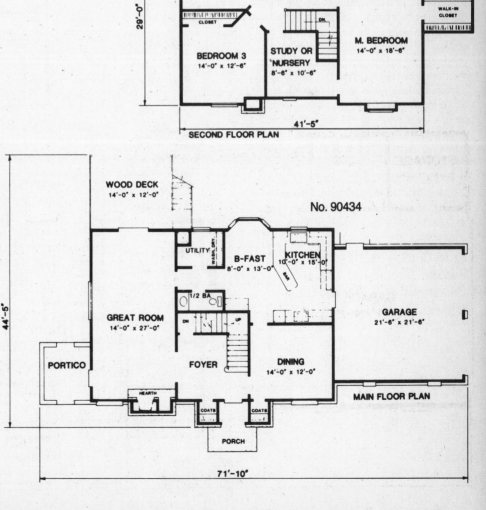

Colonial Charmer Fit for a Crowd

No. 20101

Imagine entertaining in this spacious masterpiece! Throw open the double doors between the front parlor and fire-placed family room and you've got an expansive room that can handle any crowd. There's room for an army of cooks in the bayed kitchen-breakfast room combination. And, when the oven overheats the room, head out to the adjoining deck for a breath of fresh air. Store extra supplies in the room-sized pantry on the way to the elegant, formal dining room. The adjacent breezeway contains a handy powder room and laundry facilities. Four bedrooms are tucked upstairs, away from the action. Look at the magnificent master suite. Recessed ceilings, a skylit shower, and double vanities make this room both luxurious and convenient.

First floor — 1,109 sq. ft.
Second floor — 932 sq. ft.
Basement — 1,109 sq. ft.
Garage — 552 sq. ft.

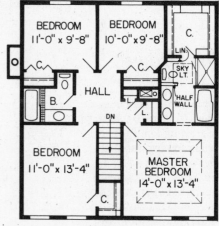

A Karl Kreeger Design

SECOND FLOOR

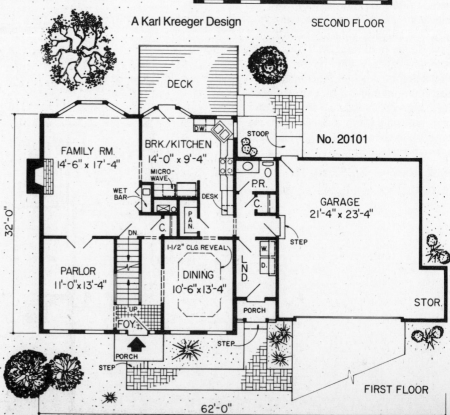

No. 20101

FIRST FLOOR

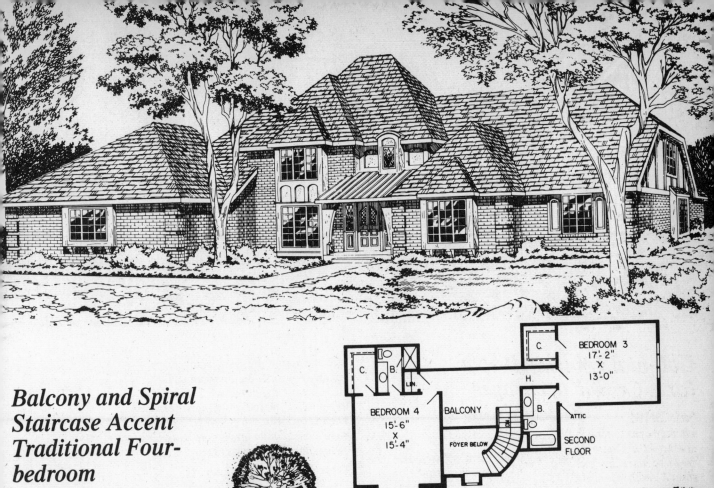

Balcony and Spiral Staircase Accent Traditional Four-bedroom

No. 10537

This roomy kitchen comes complete with pantry and lots of cabinet space. The unique morning room is complemented with a large fireplace and an entry onto the patio for year 'round enjoyment. All four bedrooms are complete with full baths and walk-in closets.

First floor — 3,114 sq. ft.
Second floor — 924 sq. ft.
Basement — 3,092 sq. ft.
Garage — 917 sq. ft.

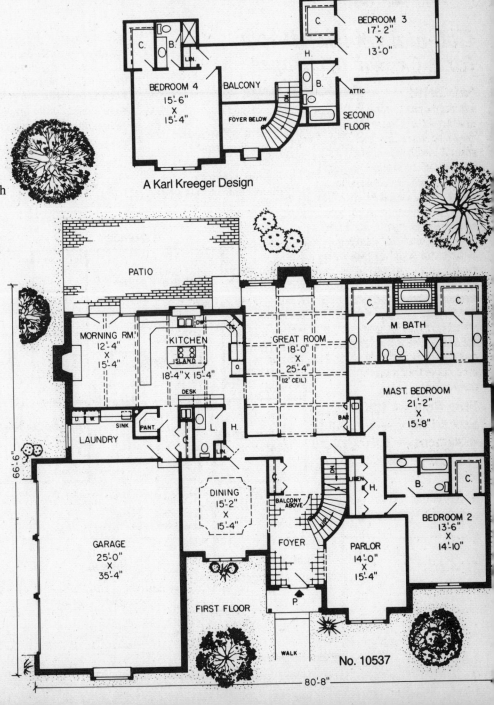

A Karl Kreeger Design

No. 10537

Living Room Encourages Entertaining

No. 9846

Radiating all the charm and welcome of a French country home, this four bedroom design is highlighted by a generously proportioned living room with fireplace. Its sliding glass doors connect to the ter- race and permit open, enjoyable enter- taining. A formal dining room and kitchen with laundry space border the living room and the set-off family room. The master bedroom enjoys a bath and huge closet, while three more bedrooms and another bath are included.

First floor — 2,022 sq. ft.
Basement — 2,022 sq. ft.
Garage — 576 sq. ft.

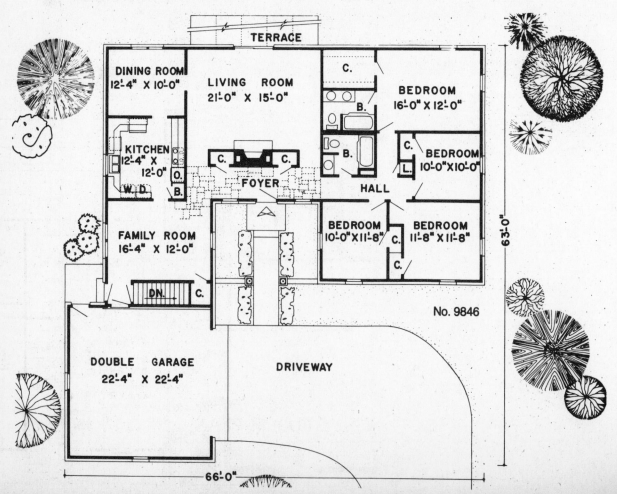

TERRACE

DINING ROOM 12'-4" X 10'-0"

LIVING ROOM 21'-0" X 15'-0"

C.

BEDROOM 16'-0" X 12'-0"

KITCHEN 12'-4" X 12'-0"

B.

B.

C.

BEDROOM 10'-0" X 10'-0"

L.

W.D.

B.

C.   C.

FOYER

HALL

FAMILY ROOM 16'-4" X 12'-0"

BEDROOM 10'-0" X 11'-8"

C.

BEDROOM 11'-8" X 11'-8"

C.

63'-0"

DN.   C.

No. 9846

DOUBLE GARAGE 22'-4" X 22'-4"

DRIVEWAY

66'-0"

New England Tradition

No. 90608

This salt box classic appeals to almost everyone. It copies the best from the Colonial residential tradition and adds modern conveniences and efficiencies. A spacious foyer channels traffic to all parts of the house. The large, U-shaped kitchen serves the dinette, dining room, and patio. The ground floor bedroom can be easily adapted as a den; note the two entrances to the bath. Three bedrooms on the 2nd floor have plenty of closet space. The master bedroom has a walk-in closet and plush bath.

First floor — 1,132 sq.ft.
Second floor — 840 sq.ft.

SECOND FLOOR PLAN

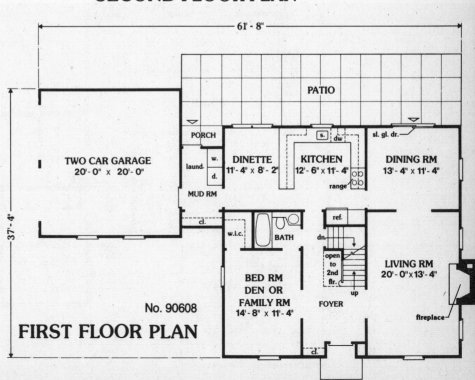

No. 90608

FIRST FLOOR PLAN

Outdoor-Lovers' Delight

No. 10748

This one-level charmer packs a lot of convenience into a compact space. From the shelter of the front porch, the foyer leads three ways: right to the bedroom wing, left to the roomy kitchen and dining room, or straight ahead to the massive living room. You'll appreciate the quiet atmosphere in the sleeping wing, the elegant recessed ceilings and private bath in the master suite, and the laundry facilities that adjoin the bedrooms. You'll enjoy the convenience of a kitchen with a built-in pantry and adjacent dining room. And, you'll love the airy atmosphere in the sunny, fireplaced living room, which features a cooling fan, high ceilings, and double French doors to the huge, wrap-around porch.

Main living area — 1,540 sq. ft.
Porches — 530 sq. ft.

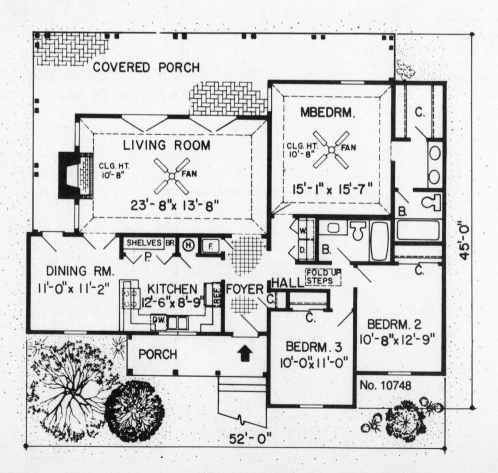

Two-Story Tile Foyer Welcomes Guests and Family Alike

No. 10501

Make a wonderful first impression or return home to this massive, welcoming foyer and step right into the great room of this tastefully appointed design. The great room is enlarged by a wrap-around deck and highlighted by a fireplace, built-in bookcases and wetbar. The first floor master suite is equally inviting with its spacious dressing area and separate bath. Adjacent to the central great room, the kitchen area has its own built-in desk, octagonal morning room and central island. The second floor includes three bedrooms linked by a balcony which overlooks the great room and the open foyer.

First floor — 2,419 sq. ft.
Second floor — 926 sq. ft.
Garage — 615 sq. ft.
Basement — 2,419 sq. ft.

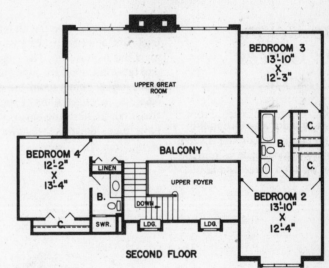

SECOND FLOOR

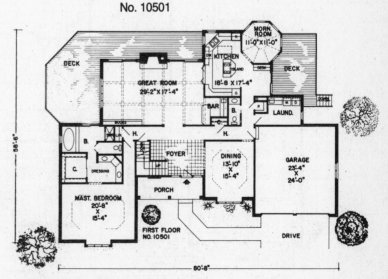

No. 10501

A Karl Kreeger Design

Floor-to-Ceiling Window Graces Formal Parlor

No. 20080

There's a taste of tudor elegance in this three-bedroom family home. You'll see it in the brick and stucco facade with rustic wood trim, in the tiled foyer, and in the fireplaced family room with ten foot ceilings. But, it's easy to see how convenient this plan is, too. The island kitchen and breakfast nook are adjacent to a gracious formal dining room and outdoor deck, perfect for a summer supper. The first-floor master suite means you won't have to trek down the stairs for your morning coffee. The kids will love their upstairs bath. A skylight assures privacy and a sunny atmosphere.

First floor — 1,859 sq. ft.
Second floor — 556 sq. ft.
Basement — 1,844 sq. ft.
Garage — 598 sq. ft.

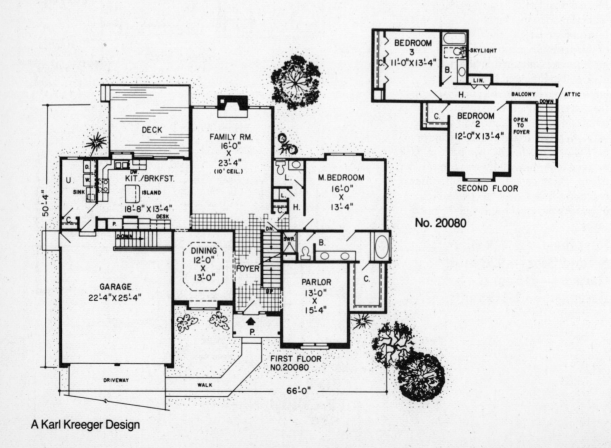

No. 20080

A Karl Kreeger Design

Wide-Open and Convenient

No. 20100

Stacked windows fill the wall in the front bedroom of this one-level home, creating an attractive facade, and a sunny atmosphere inside. Around the corner, two more bedrooms and two full baths complete the bedroom wing, set apart for bedtime quiet. Notice the elegant vaulted ceiling in the master bedroom, the master tub and shower illuminated by a skylight, and the double vanities in both baths. Active areas enjoy a spacious feeling. Look at the high, sloping ceilings in the fireplaced living room, the sliders that unite the breakfast room and kitchen with an adjoining deck, and the vaulted ceilings in the formal dining room off the foyer.

Main floor — 1,727 sq. ft.
Basement — 1,727 sq. ft.
Garage — 484 sq. ft.

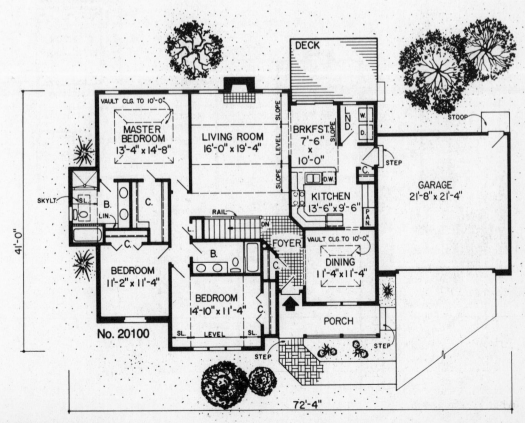

A Karl Kreeger Design

Porch Adorns Elegant Bay

No. 20093

Here's a compact Victorian charmer that unites tradition with today in a perfect combination. Imagine waking up in the roomy master suite with its romantic bay and full bath with double sinks. Two additional bedrooms, which feature huge closets, share the hall bath. The romance continues in the sunny breakfast room off the island kitchen, in the recessed ceilings of the formal dining room, and in the living room's cozy fireplace. Sun lovers will appreciate the sloping, skylit ceilings in the living room, and the rear deck accessible from both the kitchen and living room.

First floor — 978 sq. ft.
Second floor — 812 sq. ft.
Basement — 978 sq. ft.

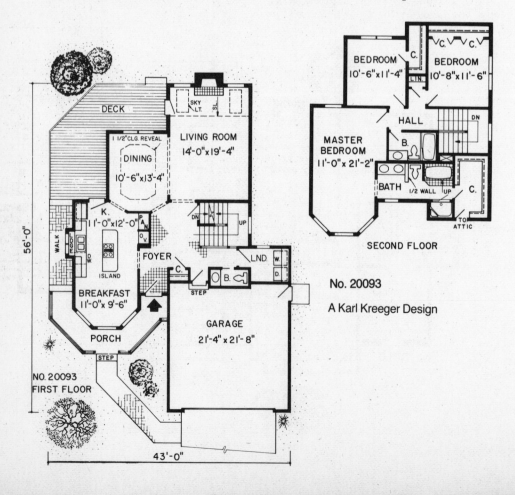

No. 20093

A Karl Kreeger Design

Four-bedroom Design Offers Lots of Living Space

No. 10461

Good use of available space places three bedrooms in one front area of this efficiently designed home. The master suite on the other side incorporates a walk-in closet plus a large bath accented by a skylight. The tiled family room has a wetbar and looks out onto the patio through a wall of glass. The living room also has a lovely view of the patio and is further enhanced by a fireplace and a built-in bookcase. The dining room is adjacent to the living room and to the kitchen's breakfast nook. The kitchen features plenty of storage and a compact work triangle.

Living Area — 2,102 sq. ft.
Garage — 493 sq. ft.

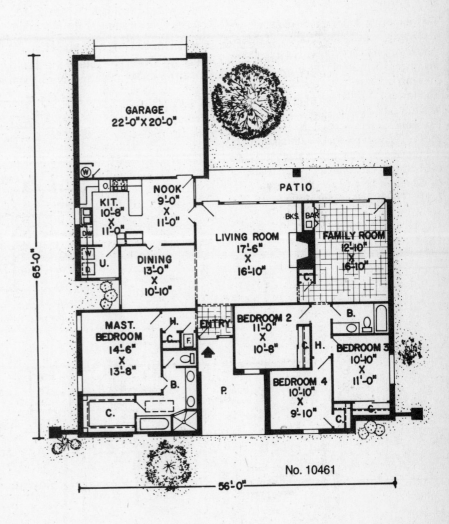

No. 10461

Stately Tudor

No. 90002

This imposing and impressive facade was designed to satisfy the scrutiny of those who love English details. The eye-catching tower soars above the main roof, housing a dramatic interior stair foyer. The tower is further enhanced by a bay window, shed roofs, dormers, open timber work, and truncated, gabled, and hip roofs. The carved double-entrance doors are flanked by iron grilled side lights. A dual closet vestibule greets guests and flows into a 11 x 13 ft. curved-stair foyer. The living room is large and impressive with its 9 foot high window, 7 foot wide window seat, log burning fireplace with 13 foot hearth, and double French doors leading to the rear porch.

First floor — 1,679 sq. ft.
Second floor — 1,040 sq. ft.

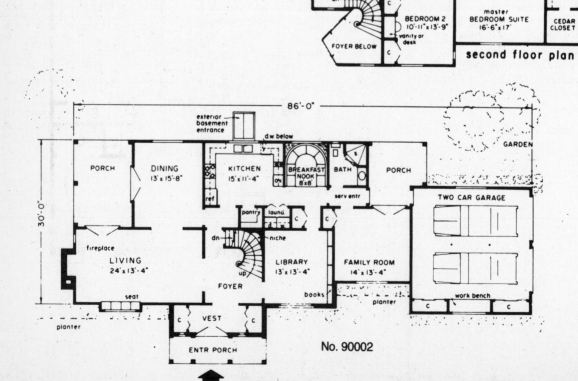

first floor plan

Energy Efficient

No. 90130

Choose either a single or double garage to complement this compact, three bedroom home plan. Lots of living is packed into this space conscious design which is organized around the multipurpose great room. This extra large living area accommodates all of the family's activities by making the galley style kitchen an integral part of the living space. Another advantage of the room arrangement is seen in the separation of the living area from the three bedrooms. This separation is achieved through the placement of the two full baths and of the closets.

Living area — 1,118 sq. ft.

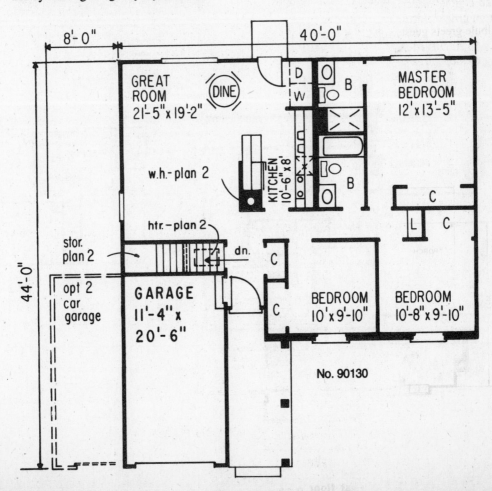

No. 90130

Room for Family Activities

No. 10649

With two covered porches and a brick patio, this traditional Cape is an inviting abode for your outdoor-loving family. The central entry leads down a hallway to the family room. Warmed by a fireplace and boasting a wet bar, lots of windows and french doors, this enormous room is a great gathering place. Serve meals in the bay-windowed breakfast nook or the formal dining room located on either side of the kitchen. Window seats adorning the front bedrooms upstairs provide a pleasant retreat for quiet moments.

First floor — 1,285 sq. ft.
Second floor — 930 sq. ft.
Garage — 492 sq. ft.

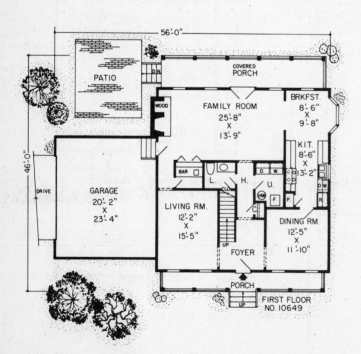

Timeless Elegance

No. 20105

The handsome tudor exterior of this four-bedroom classic is mirrored by an exciting interior plan of extraordinary beauty. Step through the foyer, flanked by a formal dining room and library, and past the stairway to a massive living room characterized by high ceilings, abundant windows, and access to a private rear deck. With two-way access to the bar and fireplace, both living and hearth rooms share easy entertaining and a cozy atmosphere. The adjoining kitchen, with its handy breakfast bar and nearby pantry, is a marvel of convenience. Look at the recessed ceilings, twin walk-in closets, and luxurious bath in the first-floor master suite. Upstairs, three ample bedrooms enjoy walk-in closets and adjoining baths.

First floor — 2,080 sq. ft.
Second floor — 1,051 sq. ft.
Basement — 2,080 sq. ft.
Garage — 666 sq. ft.

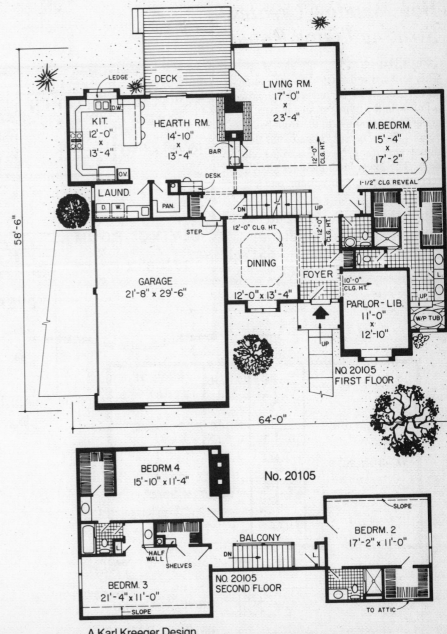

A Karl Kreeger Design

Bow Window Creates Striking Living Room

No. 9310

This split-foyer design has a very attractive facade which includes a large bow window in the living room and two square bay windows in the front bedrooms. The efficient kitchen joins the dining area for direct access to the rear deck. The lower level includes a large recreation room, utility room, and a workshop.

Upper level — 1,461 sq. ft.
Lower level — 740 sq. ft.
Garage and workshop — 651 sq. ft.

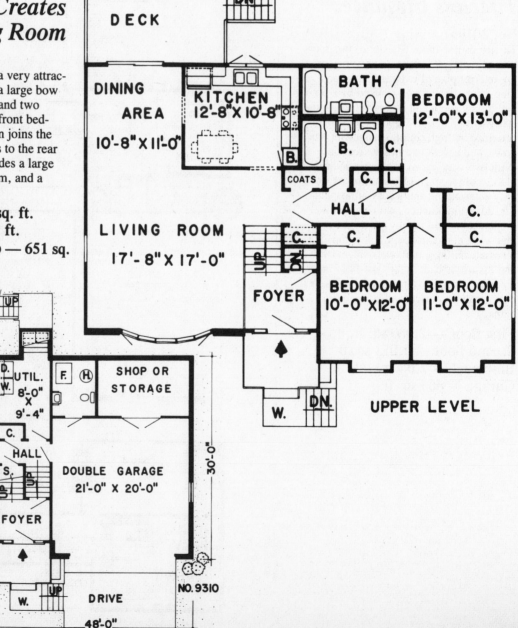

Entry Hints at Appealing Interior

No. 10678

Interesting angles give every room in this three-bedroom home a distinctive shape. Stand in the foyer and look up. Soaring ceilings in the window-walled living room rise to dizzying heights. Step past the powder room to find a fireplaced family room, wide open to the convenient kitchen with built-in desk and pantry. Just outside, there's lots of warm weather living space on the deck surrounding the dining room. Walk upstairs to the vaulted den that links the bedrooms and provides a comfortable spot for enjoying a good book. And, look at the adjoining deck! Can't you imagine perching up there on a sunny day, watching the world go by?

First floor — 1,375 sq. ft.
Second floor — 1,206 sq. ft.
Basement — 1,375 sq. ft.

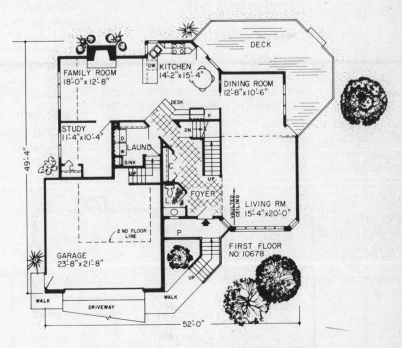

No. 10678   A Design by William E. Gage

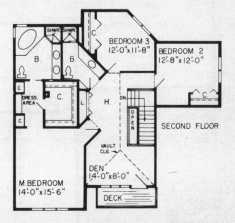

Designed for Entertaining

No. 10587

The double doors of the vaulted entry are just a hint of the graceful touches in this three-bedroom home. Curves soften the stairway, deck, and the huge bar that runs between the formal and informal dining areas. Skylights, bay-, and bump-out windows flood every room with light. And when the sun goes down, you can keep things cozy with fireplaces in the family and sunken living rooms. For a quiet retreat, sneak upstairs to deck off the master bedroom suite.

First floor — 2,036 sq. ft.
Second floor — 1,554 sq. ft.
Garage — 533 sq. ft.

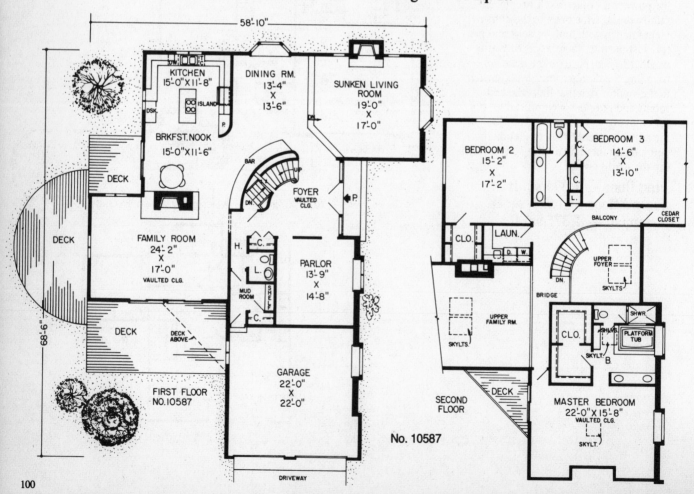

Modified Cape for Family Living

No. 10634

With a graceful porch sheltering three sides of this inviting abode, and a patio off the back, you can enjoy all your summer evenings outside. Walk out for a breath of fresh air after a full meal in the formal dining room or sunny breakfast nook. The adjoining kitchen and cozy family room are located across the central foyer from the spacious living room. Sharing the second floor with three bedrooms and two baths, the master suite features a hexagonal sitting room.

First floor — 1,412 sq. ft.
Second floor — 1,382 sq. ft.

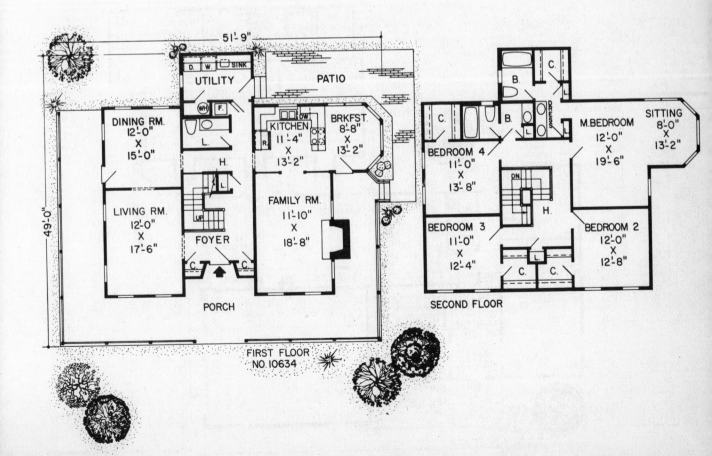

Steeped in Tradition

No. 10628

This inviting home meets the needs of the modern family with the warmth of a traditional design. Classic touches include shutter-trimmed, double-hung windows, clapboard and brick siding, and a central entry flanked by side lights. Beamed ceilings, a cozy fireplace flanked by built-in bookcases, and a romantic window seat lend old-world charm to the family room. A separate, formal parlor and quiet den removed from the bustle of the house are pleasant reminders of another time. But, the open, L-shaped arrangement of the island kitchen, formal dining and family rooms, the abundant closet space throughout the house, and the luxury of a walk-in shower and raised tub in the master suite are amenities that make this three-bedroom charmer a home for today.

First floor — 1,757 sq. ft.
Second floor — 1075 sq. ft.
Basement — 1,757 sq. ft.

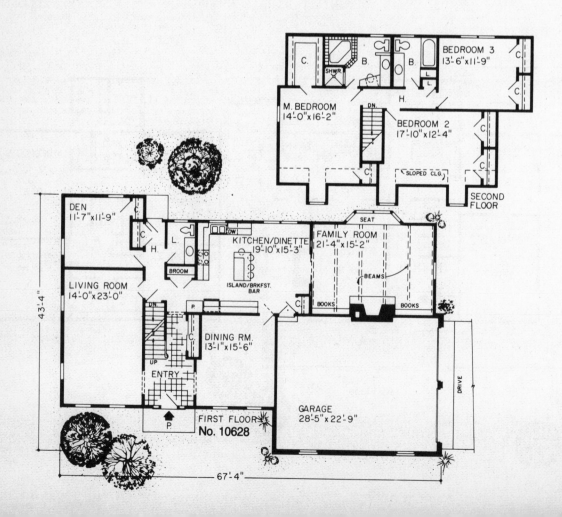

Traditional Warmth

No. 90817

Here is a country charmer with a cozy feeling. A wrap-around front porch shelters the front door, which opens to a central foyer and a view of the living room and patio. Both living and family rooms feature back to back fieldstone fireplaces. The pantried kitchen and dining area are conveniently connected. With three large bedrooms and two full baths upstairs, this home has plenty of room for a growing family.

Main floor — 1,161 sq. ft.
Second floor — 972 sq. ft.
Unfinished basement —
1,131 sq. ft.
Width — 63 ft.
Depth — 41 ft.

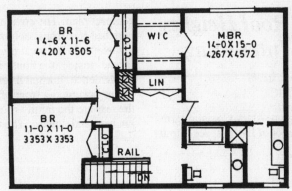

SECOND FLOOR

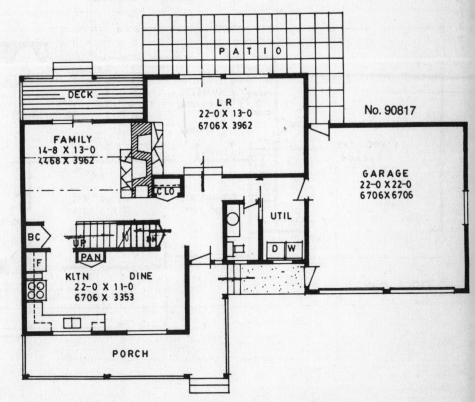

No. 90817

Varied Roof Heights Create Interesting Lines

No. 90601

This rambling one-story Colonial farmhouse packs a lot of living space into its compact plan. The covered porch, enriched by arches, columns and Colonial details, is the focal point of the facade. Inside, the house is zoned for convenience. Formal living and dining rooms occupy the front of the house. To the rear are the family room, island kitchen, and dinette. The family room features a heat-circulating fireplace, visible from the entrance foyer, and sliding glass doors to the large rear patio. Three bedrooms and two baths are away from the action in a private wing.

Total living area — 1,536 sq. ft. (Optional slab construction available)

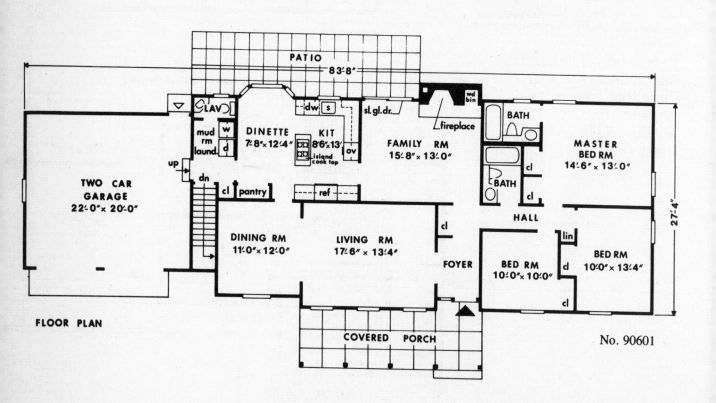

FLOOR PLAN

No. 90601

Deluxe Master Suite Includes Garden Tub

00400

This stately English Tudor design features a downstairs master suite with one walk-in plus two additional closets and a compartmentalized bath with double vanity, garden tub and separate shower. The formal foyer is flanked by a dining room on one side and a living room on the other. For more casual living, a sunken family room with a raised-hearth fire-place, wet bar and a half bath is included. The spacious kitchen with breakfast nook and a large utility room with a laundry chute from upstairs complete the main floor. An open stairwell leads to the upper level which includes your choice of a large study or a two story foyer. Also located on the upper level are three bedrooms with generous closet space including two walk-in closets, two more compartmentalized baths and a linen closet and laundry chute to the utility room. All or part of the basement can be used to supplement the main living area. Specify basement or crawlspace foundation when ordering.

First floor — 1,759 sq. ft.
Second floor — 1,269 sq. ft.

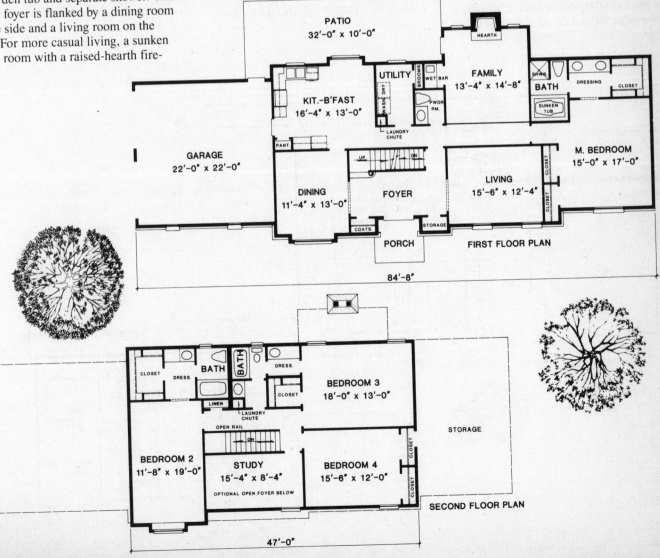

Gingerbread Charm

No. 10690

Victorian elegance combines with a modern floor plan to make this a dream house without equal. A wrap-around porch and rear deck add lots of extra living space to the roomy first floor, which features a formal parlor and dining room just off the central entry. Informal areas at the rear of the house are wide-open for family interaction. Gather the crew around the fireplace in the family room, or make supper in the kitchen while you supervise the kids' homework in the sunwashed breakfast room. Three bedrooms, tucked upstairs for a quiet atmosphere, feature skylit baths. And, you'll love the five-sided sitting nook in your master suite, a perfect spot to relax after a luxurious bath in the sunken tub.

First floor — 1,260 sq. ft.
Second floor — 1,021 sq. ft.
Basement — 1,186 sq. ft.
Garage — 840 sq. ft.

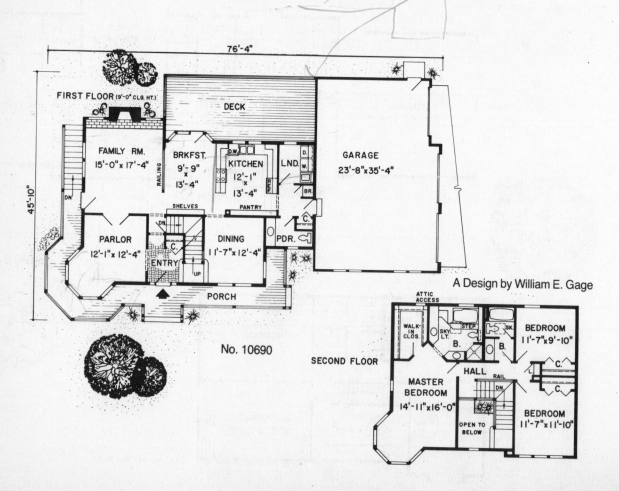

A Design by William E. Gage

No. 10690

Enjoy a Crackling Fire on a Chilly Day

No. 10683

From the dramatic, two-story entry to the full-length deck off the massive great room, this is a modern plan in a classic package. Cathedral ceilings soar over the formal dining and sunken living rooms, separated by an open railing. The corner kitchen efficiently serves formal and family eating areas. Can't you imagine a table overlooking the deck in the sunken great room's sunny bay? Up the angular staircase, two bedrooms, each with a huge closet, share a full bath. You'll have your own, private bath, including double vanities and a sun-washed raised tub, in the master suite at the rear of the house.

First floor — 990 sq. ft.
Second floor — 721 sq. ft.
Basement — 934 sq. ft.
Garage — 429 sq. ft.

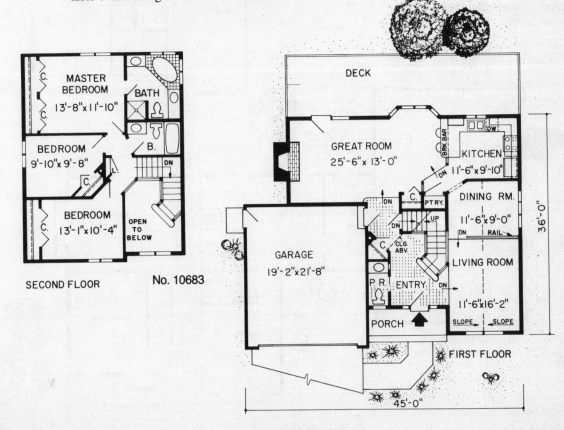

A Design by William E. Gage

Bay Window Brightens Dining Room

No. 90703

Don't worry about getting wet on a rainy day. You're protected from the car to the kitchen by the three car garage and laundry wing. The front entry, flanked by a cheerful dining room and cozy living room, is sheltered by a columned porch. Four bedrooms and two baths at the top of the central staircase allow lots of space for a growing family.

First floor — 1,171 sq. ft.
Second floor — 965 sq. ft.

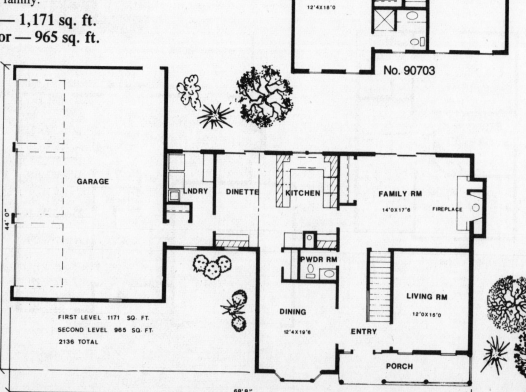

BEDRM
12'4X11'6

BATH

BEDRM
12'0X11'6

M SUITE
12'4X18'0

BEDRM
15'0X12'0

No. 90703

GARAGE

44'0"

LNDRY

DINETTE

KITCHEN

FAMILY RM
14'0X17'6

FIREPLACE

FIRST LEVEL 1171 SQ. FT.
SECOND LEVEL 965 SQ. FT.
2136 TOTAL

PWDR RM

DINING
12'4X19'6

ENTRY

LIVING RM
12'0X15'0

PORCH

68'8"

108

Handsome Design Highlighted by Multiple Windows and Interesting Roof Line

No. 10440

This story-and-a-half design organizes living areas for both privacy and convenient access. The second floor bedrooms are ideal for growing teenagers. Each has lots of closet space and the shared bathroom includes a double vanity. There's even a separate gameroom on the second floor for entertaining friends. The master bedroom is secluded from the rest of the first floor and features individual walk-in closets and dressing areas. The living areas of this home are gathered around the central entry. The large kitchen is between the formal dining room and the combination breakfast-family room. The living room has a hearthed fireplace and its own wetbar. There's even a separate study for quiet relaxation.

First floor — 2,073 sq. ft.
Second floor — 834 sq. ft.
Garage — 462 sq. ft.
Porch & Patio — 138 sq. ft.

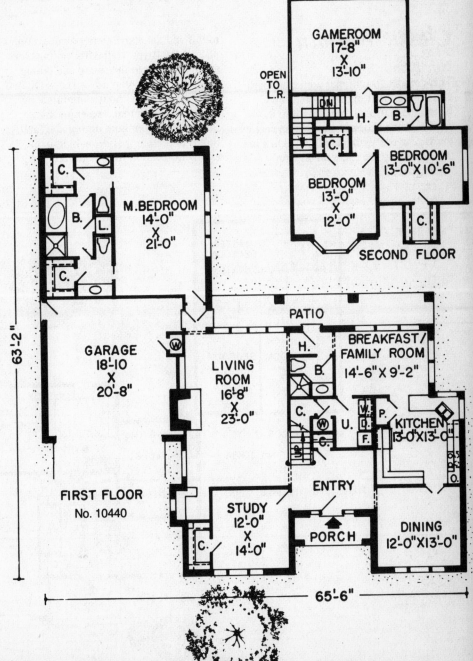

Classic Warmth

No. 10684

This compact traditional with clapboard exterior and inviting, sheltered entry boasts loads of features that make it a special home. Look at the built-in seat by the garage entry, the handy breakfast bar that separates the kitchen and family room, and the convenient powder room just off the foyer. Cathedral ceilings lend an airy quality to the living and dining rooms. A single step down keeps the two rooms separate without compromising the open feeling that's so enjoyable. Sliders lead from both dining and family rooms to the rear patio, making it an excellent location for an outdoor party.

Tucked upstairs, the three bedrooms include your own, private master suite.

First floor — 940 sq. ft.
Second floor — 720 sq. ft.
Walkout basement — 554 sq. ft.
Garage — 418 sq. ft.
Crawl space — 312 sq. ft.

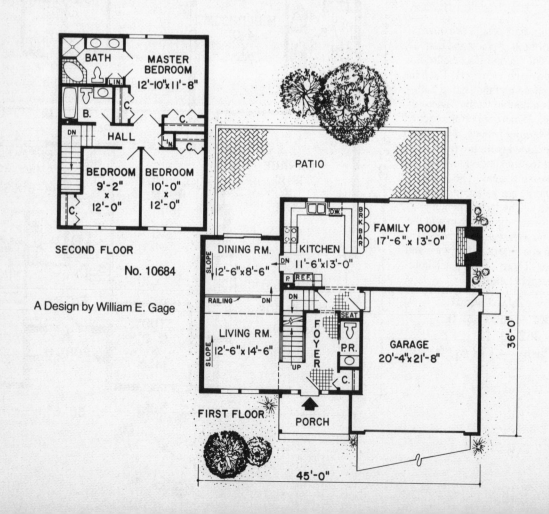

SECOND FLOOR

No. 10684

A Design by William E. Gage

Two-Story Window Flanked By Stone Dominates Facade

No. 10494

The tiled foyer leads conveniently leads to the upper two bedrooms, the master bedroom, and the central living room. A corner built-in bookcase, fireplace and dramatic window wall complete this gracious room. The front dining room, enhanced by natural lighting, is convenient to the kitchen and adjacent breakfast nook.

First floor — 1,584 sq. ft.
Second floor — 599 sq. ft.
Garage — 514 sq. ft.
Basement — 1,584 sq. ft.

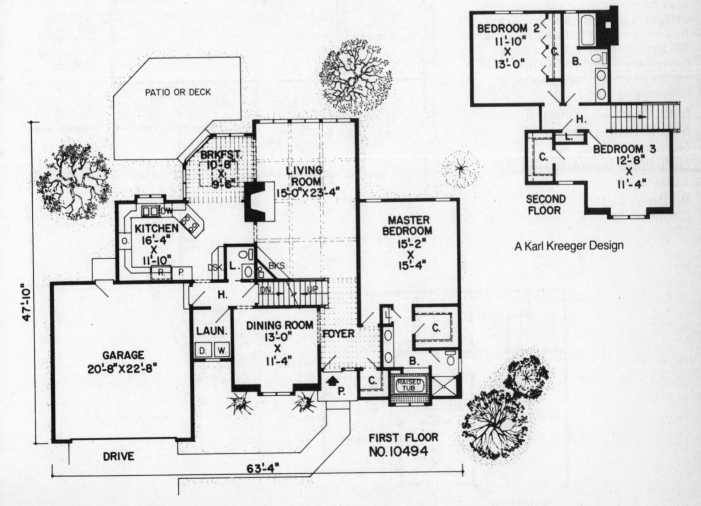

A Karl Kreeger Design

A Hint of Victorian Nostalgia

No. 90909

High roofs, tower bays, and long, railed porches give this efficient plan an old-fashioned charm that's hard to resist. The foyer opens on a classic center stairwell, wrapped in short halls that separate traffic without subtracting from room sizes. The highlight of this home for many homeowners is sure to be the lively kitchen with its full bay window and built-in eating table.

Main floor — 1,206 sq. ft.
Second floor — 969 sq. ft.
Garage — 471 sq. ft.
Unfinished basement — 1,206 sq. ft.
Width — 61 ft.
Depth — 44 ft.

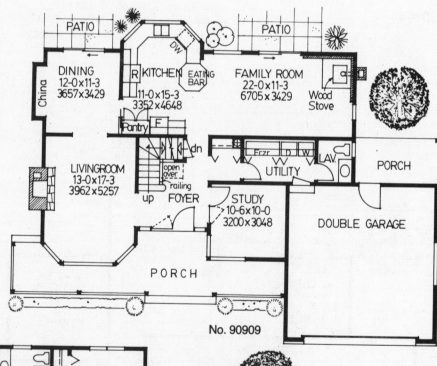

No. 90909

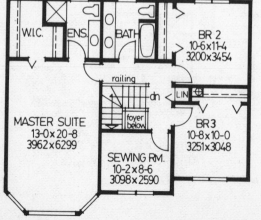

SECOND FLOOR

Balcony Affords Splendid View

No. 20097

Standing in the central foyer, you can see active areas and the rear deck off this sunny classic in one glance. Straight ahead, the living room ceiling, pierced by a skylight, soars to a two-story height. Living and dining rooms flow together in one spacious unit. And, both are easily served by the handy kitchen with a breakfast bar peninsula. Down a hallway off the living room, you'll find a quiet sleeping wing behind the garage. Two bedrooms feature access to an adjoining bath with double vanities. The second floor is all yours. Imagine stealing away for a luxurious soak in your private tub, or a relaxing afternoon with your favorite book.

First floor — 1,752 sq. ft.
Second floor — 897 sq. ft.
Basement — 1,752 sq. ft.
Garage — 531 sq. ft.

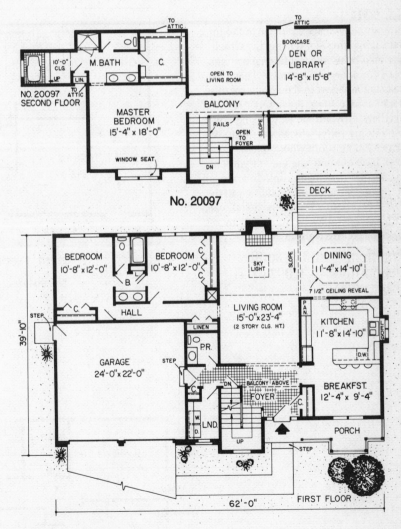

No. 20097

A Karl Kreeger Design

Country Kitchen Accents Design

No. 90119

Joining the U-shaped kitchen to the informal dining area is a serving bar which may also be used as additional counter space for a larger work area. These two areas are adjacent to the family room so there's ample space for family get-togethers. Toward the front of the house is the living room which opens onto the formal dining room whose double windows look out onto the yard or garden. The second floor bedrooms are arranged around a central bath. In addition to the master bedroom's private bath and walk-in closet, one other bedroom also incorporates a roomy walk-in closet.

First floor — 1,104 sq. ft.
Second floor — 1,092 sq. ft.

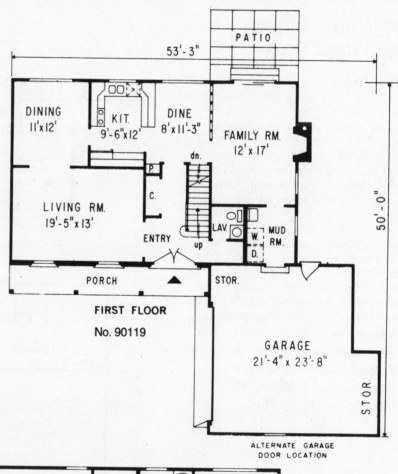

PATIO

53'-3"

DINING 11'x12'

KIT. 9'-6"x12'

DINE 8'x11'-3"

FAMILY RM. 12'x17'

50'-0"

dn.

P.

C.

LIVING RM. 19'-5"x13'

LAV.

MUD RM.

W. D.

ENTRY

up

PORCH

STOR.

FIRST FLOOR

No. 90119

GARAGE 21'-4" x 23'-8"

STOR.

ALTERNATE GARAGE
DOOR LOCATION

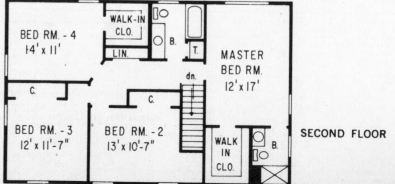

BED RM. - 4 14'x11'

WALK-IN CLO.

LIN.

B.

T.

MASTER BED RM. 12'x17'

C.

dn.

C.

BED RM. - 3 12'x11'-7"

BED RM. - 2 13'x10'-7"

WALK IN CLO.

B.

SECOND FLOOR

114

Romantic French Provincial

No. 90023

The romance of the French Provincial countryside is echoed in the exterior styling of this two-story, four-bedroom plan and should delight families with a taste for continental design. Its eye-catching character is derived from the curved window heads, angular bays, brick quoins at all corners of the brick veneer, steep roofs, and the diamond paned, copper-roofed picture bay over the double-door recessed entrance. The circular staircase with wrought iron railing provides a luxurious access to the four bedrooms on the second floor. You'll enjoy the details which retain the good qualities and hospitality of an earlier era.

First floor — 1,900 sq. ft.
Second floor — 1,692 sq. ft.
Garage — 576 sq. ft.
Basement — 1,725 sq. ft.

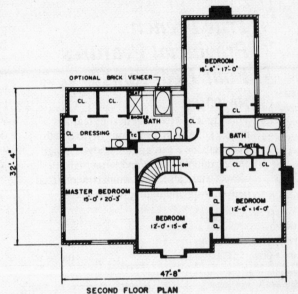

SECOND FLOOR PLAN

No. 90023

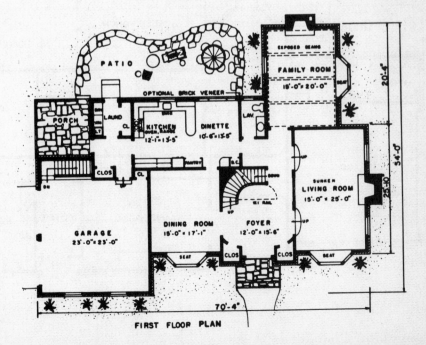

FIRST FLOOR PLAN

True French Provincial Features Four Bedrooms

No. 90408

This French Provincial design features a master suite with a spacious deluxe bath that includes a garden tub, shower, linen closet, double vanity and large walk-in closets share a second compartmentalized bath. Living and dining rooms are located to the side of the formal foyer. Both the family room, with fireplace and double doors opening onto a screened-in back porch, and a U-shaped kitchen, with an island counter open to the break-fast bay, allow more casual living. Fixed stairs in the family room provide access to attic storage above. Also included is a utility room with a half bath.

Area — 2,968 sq. ft.

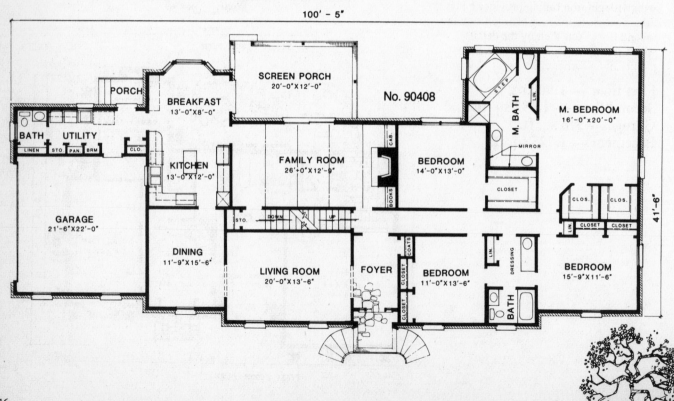

Warm and Inviting

No. 90827

Here's a traditional design for your growing family, complete with a rainy day porch and a second floor sitting area with a romantic balcony. The entry is flanked by a formal sunken living room and cozy family room. At mealtime, choose the formal dining room or the sunny, pleasant breakfast room off the kitchen. And, don't worry about tracking mud through your clean house. Deposit your boots and other items in the utility room by the back door. Three bedrooms, including the spacious master suite, share the second floor with the open sitting area and an adjoining study.

First floor — 1,349 sq. ft.
Second floor — 1,199 sq. ft.
Unfinished basement — 1,349 sq. ft.

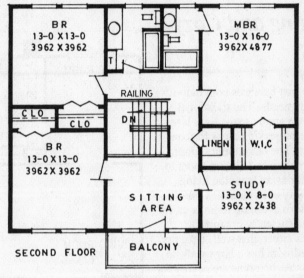

SECOND FLOOR

BR 13-0 X 13-0 3962 X 3962

MBR 13-0 X 16-0 3962 X 4877

CLO   CLO

RAILING

DN

BR 13-0 X 13-0 3962 X 3962

LINEN   W.I.C

STUDY 13-0 X 8-0 3962 X 2438

SITTING AREA

BALCONY

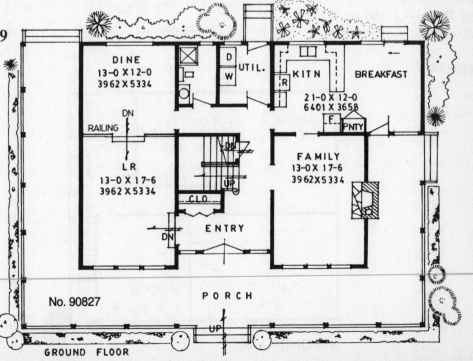

GROUND FLOOR

No. 90827

DINE 13-0 X 12-0 3962 X 5334

UTIL.

KITN

BREAKFAST 21-0 X 12-0 6401 X 3658

DN

RAILING

LR 13-0 X 17-6 3962 X 5334

CLO

FAMILY 13-0 X 17-6 3962 X 5334

PNTY

UP

DN

ENTRY

PORCH

UP

Charming and Cozy Rooms

No. 90126

Here a home that balances both individual and family needs. The traditional design encloses ample space for a large family, while preserving areas for comfort and quiet. The large family room, with cozy fireplace and sliding doors to the patio, is far away from the living room to simplify entertaining. Complementing the formal dining room is an eat-in nook. The efficiently organized kitchen serves either area well. Upstairs, the master bedroom has a large walk-in closet. Two other berooms are nearby for nighttime security.

First floor — 1,260 sq. ft.
Second floor — 952 sq. ft.

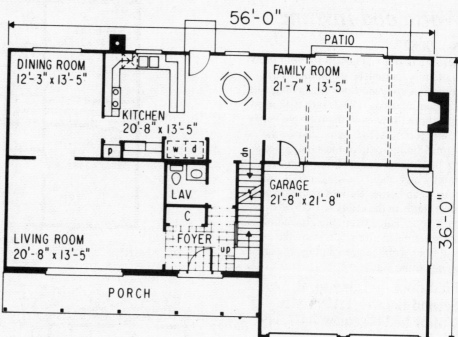

No. 90126

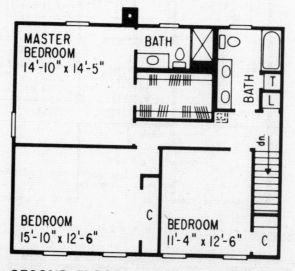

SECOND FLOOR

One-Floor Living, Tudor Style

No. 20099

You'll find an appealing quality of open space in every room of this unique one-level home. Angular windows and recessed ceilings separate the two dining rooms from the adjoining island kitchen without compromising the airy feeling. A window-wall that flanks the fireplace in the soaring, skylit living room unites interior spaces with the outdoor deck. The sunny atmosphere continues in the master suite, with its bump-out window and double-vanitied bath, and in the two bedrooms off the foyer.

First floor — 2,020 sq. ft.
Basement — 2,020 sq. ft.
Garage — 534 sq. ft.

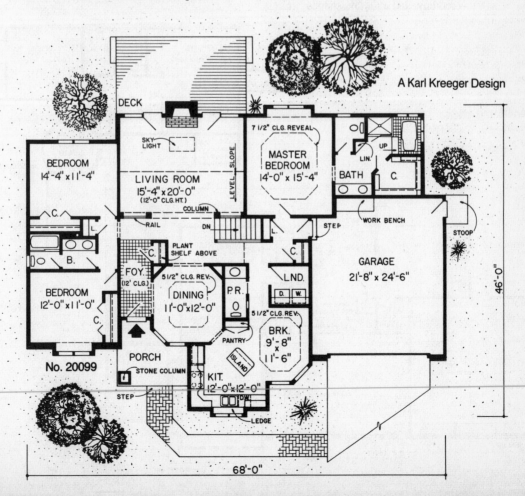

Modest Tudor With A Massive Look

No. 90012

Specifically designed to make its presence felt in any neighborhood, this stately Tudor home contains fewer square feet, and is more affordable, than one would imagine. Broken and steeply sloping roof lines, dormers, a large cantilevered bay, and a Gothic shaped, unique entrance way —as well as the charming stone, brick, and half-timber materials— all add keen interest to the exterior. The living/dining space is an open 34 ft. area designed to be an impressive focal point; a large log burning fireplace is centrally located on the far wall. The triple windows in the front allow for a grand view.

First floor — 1,078 sq. ft.
Second floor — 1,131 sq. ft.

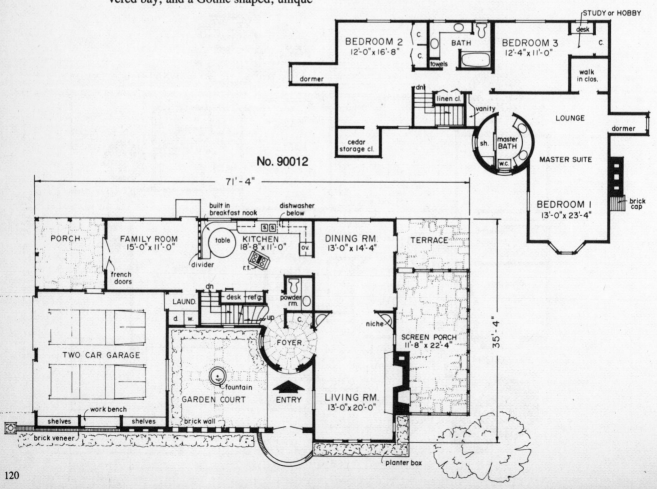

No. 90012

Luxury, Beauty and Warmth

No. 9292

Native stone, antique brick, and white siding and trim are skillfully blended together on the front of this house for a beautiful exterior. The house appears much larger than it actually is, yet you'll clean and heat only 1,366 square feet.

The floor plan shows three bedrooms and two full baths. The master bedroom is nicely proportioned and has a large walk-in closet. The garage is extra large and has additional storage areas.

First floor — 1,366 sq. ft.
Garage — 619 sq. ft.
Basement — 1,366 sq. ft.

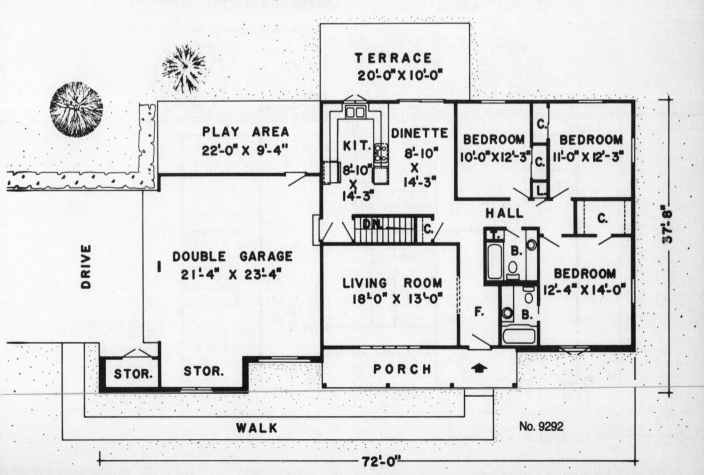

One-Level Living with a Twist

No. 20083

Here's an inviting home with a distinctive difference. Active living areas are wide-open and centrally located. From the foyer, you'll enjoy a full view of the spacious dining, living, and kitchen areas in one sweeping glance. You can even see the deck adjoining the breakfast room. The difference in this house lies in the bedrooms. Each is a private retreat, away from active areas. The master suite at the rear of the house features a full bath with double sinks. Two additional bedrooms, off in their own wing, share a full bath and the quiet atmosphere that results from intelligent design.

First floor — 1,575 sq. ft.
Basement — 1,575 sq. ft.
Garage — 475 sq. ft.

A Karl Kreeger Design

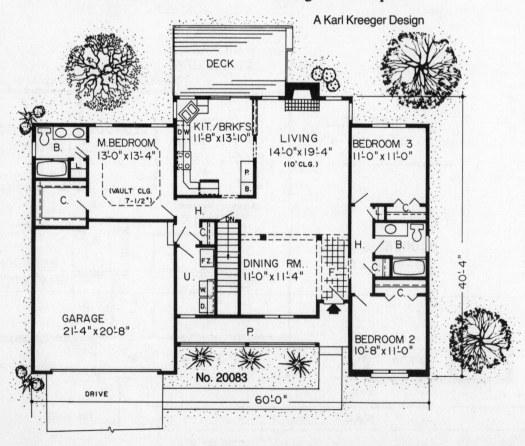

Two-Sink Baths Ease Morning Rush

No. 90622

Save energy and construction costs by building this friendly farmhouse colonial. The inviting covered porch opens to a center hall, enhanced by the stairway leading to the four-bedroom second floor. Flanked by formal living and dining rooms, the foyer leads right into the open, beamed family room, island kitchen and bay window dinette. The rear porch adjoins both family and living rooms.

First floor — 983 sq. ft.
Second floor — 1,013 sq. ft.
Mud Room — 99 sq. ft.
Garage — 481 sq. ft.
(available with or without basement)

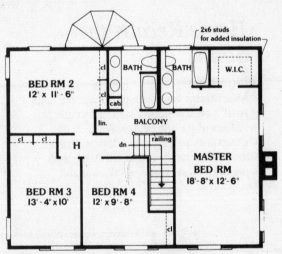

SECOND FLOOR PLAN

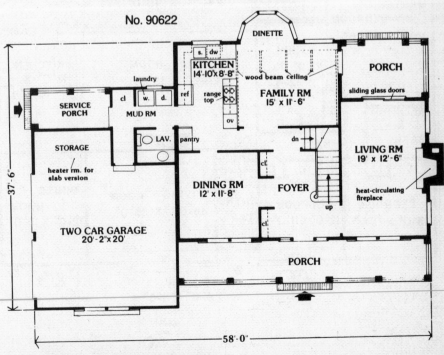

No. 90622

FIRST FLOOR PLAN

Home Recalls the South

No. 9850

Magnificent white columns, shutters, and small paned windows combine to create images of the antebellum South in this generously proportioned design. Inside, the opulent master bedroom suite, with plentiful closet space, a full bath and study, suggests modern luxury. Fireplaces enhance the formal living room and sizable family room, which skirts the lovely screened porch. The formal dining room boasts built-in china closets.

First floor — 2,466 sq. ft.
Basement — 1,447 sq. ft.
Garage — 664 sq. ft.

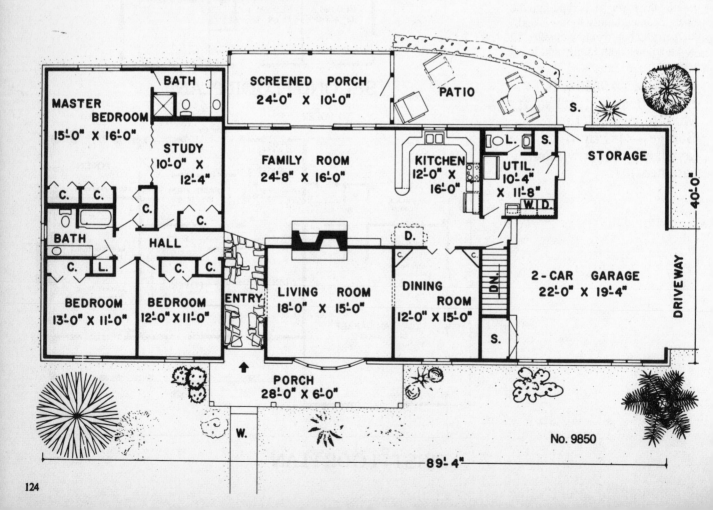

Three Private Dressing Rooms

No. 90039

The front and rear exposed living room with its log burning fireplace and covered rear porch, the double access family room, the curved walled dining room with porch entry, and kitchen providing a circular breakfast nook, planning desk and concealed laundry make up the impressive balance of the first floor. The second floor, comfortably housing three large bedrooms offers unique features: a balconied hall, three private dressing rooms, large four-fixture bath with two windows, luxurious closet space and a master bedroom suite with private bath, three rear sky windows, four front windows and a 15 x 20 foot storage room.

First floor — 1,064 sq. ft.
Second floor — 947 sq. ft.

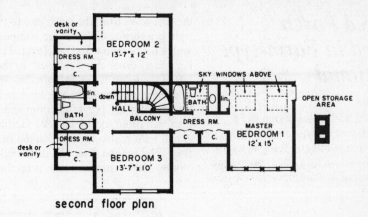

second floor plan

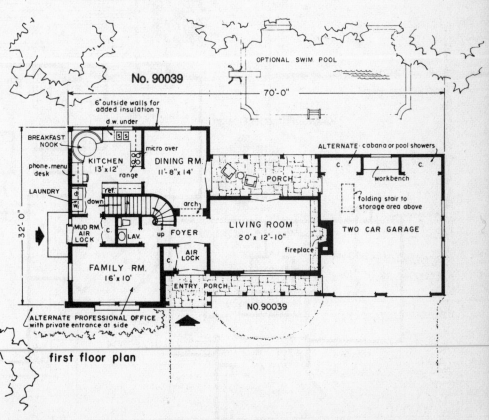

first floor plan

125

Covered Porch Offered in Farm-type Traditional

No. 20064

This pleasant traditional design has a farmhouse flavor exterior that incorporates a covered porch and features a circle wood louver on its garage, giving this design a feeling of sturdiness. Inside on the first level from the foyer and to the right is a formal dining room complete with a bay window and an elevated ceiling and a corner china cabinet. To the left of the foyer is the living room with a woodburning fireplace. The kitchen is connected to the breakfast room and there is a room for the laundry facilities. A half bath is also featured on the first floor. The second floor has three bedrooms. The master bedroom is on the second floor and has its own private bath and walk-in closet. The other two bedrooms share a full bath. A two-car garage is also added into this design.

First floor — 892 sq. ft.
Second floor — 836 sq. ft.
Basement — 892 sq. ft.
Garage — 491 sq. ft.

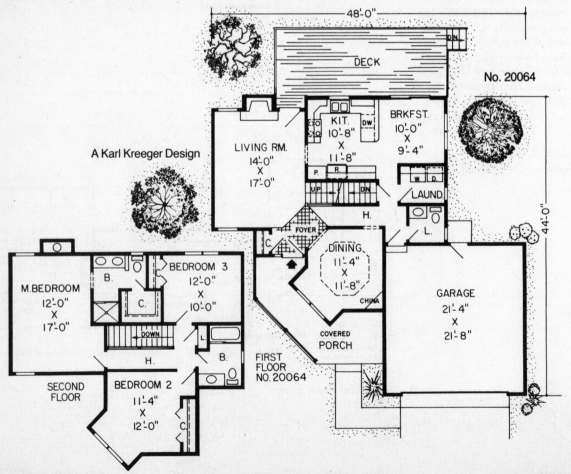

A Karl Kreeger Design

No. 20064

126

Ideal for Formal Entertaining

No. 90421

This lovely French Provincal design features a formal foyer flanked by the living room on one side and the dining room on the other. A family room with a raised-hearth fireplace and double doors to the patio, and the L-shaped island kitchen with breakfast bay and open counter to the family room allow for more casual living. Adjacent to the breakfast bay is a utility room with outside entrance. The master suite includes one double closet and a compartmentalized bath with a walk-in closet, step-up garden tub, double vanity and linen closet. Two front bedrooms and a second full bath with a linen closet complete the design. A recessed entry and circular porch add to the formal exterior.

Area — 1,940 sq. ft.

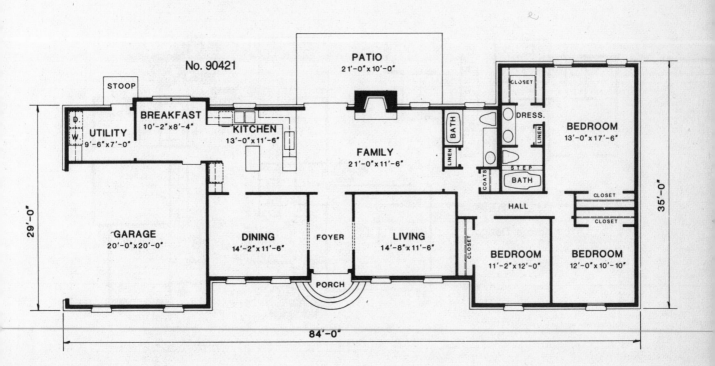

No. 90421

STOOP

PATIO
21'-0" x 10'-0"

BREAKFAST
10'-2" x 8'-4"

UTILITY
9'-6" x 7'-0"

KITCHEN
13'-0" x 11'-6"

LINEN BATH

CLOSET

DRESS.

BEDROOM
13'-0" x 17'-6"

FAMILY
21'-0" x 11'-6"

LINEN

COATS

STEP

BATH

HALL

CLOSET

CLOSET

GARAGE
20'-0" x 20'-0"

DINING
14'-2" x 11'-6"

FOYER

LIVING
14'-8" x 11'-6"

CLOSET

BEDROOM
11'-2" x 12'-0"

BEDROOM
12'-0" x 10'-10"

PORCH

29'-0"

35'-0"

84'-0"

Porch Recalls a Romantic Era

No. 20098

Arched windows and a two-story bay lend an air of elegance to this exceptional four-bedroom beauty. Interior spaces are characterized by distinctive ceiling treatments, sloping ceilings pierced by skylights, and efficient room placements.

Notice how easily the kitchen serves the hexagonal breakfast room, the formal dining room, and the adjoining deck. Even the fireplaced living room is only steps away. And, when the alarm rings early in the morning, you'll be grateful for the master suite's proximity to the coffee pot. The staircase off the foyer leads to three more bedrooms and a full, skylit bath with double vanities. Be sure to notice the wonderful angles and generous closet space in each room.

First floor — 1,843 sq. ft.
Second floor — 1039 sq. ft.
Basement — 1,843 sq. ft.
Garage — 484 sq. ft.

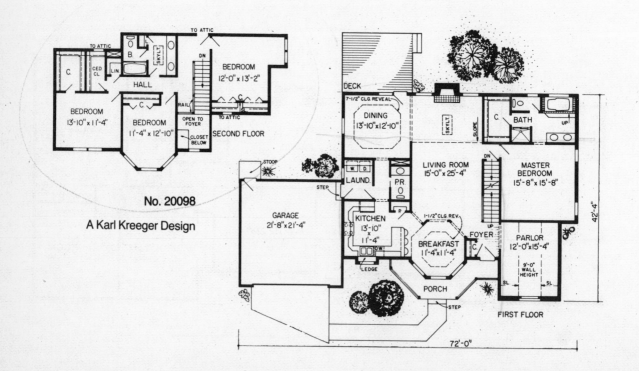

No. 20098

A Karl Kreeger Design

Touched with Tudor

No. 20088

Here's an elegant home for your growing family. With four upstairs bedrooms, each featuring a walk-in closet, there's plenty of room for everyone. And, three full baths insure the morning rush won't be a problem. Down the U-shaped stairway, a central hallway links family areas at the rear of the house with the two-story foyer and formal areas. Living and dining rooms, featuring a bump-out window and recessed ceiling, form one open space. With the island kitchen right next door, entertaining will be easy. Enjoy family meals in the breakfast room with adjoining pantry, or out on the deck. Window walls and sliders in the breakfast room and fireplaced family room unite outdoor and interior spaces for an airy feeling your family will cherish.

First floor — 1,404 sq. ft.
Second floor — 1,346 sq. ft.
Basement — 1,404 sq. ft.
Garage — 521 sq. ft.

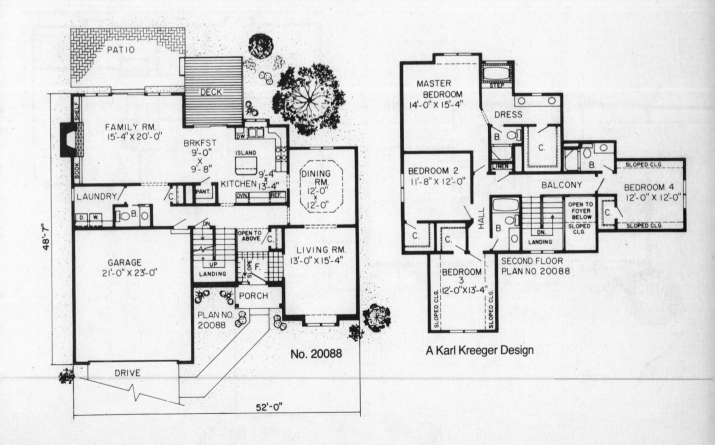

Screened Porch Offered in Dutch Colonial

No. 10576

The attractive fascade of early Dutch colonial design displays many features convenient for rearing a family. Inside on the first level, the foyer has closet space available for all weather garments. Past the foyer is the kitchen that has both informal and formal dining rooms. The living room is located next to the formal dining room and has a bay window that allows more natural lighting to the room. The family room lies to the right of the foyer and has a wood-burning fireplace. In front of the family room are sliding glass doors that lead out to a screened porch. A mud room located next to the garage is a necessity for a growing family. On the second level are four bedrooms and two spacious baths.

First floor-1,271 sq. ft.
Second floor-1,311 sq. ft.
Basement-921 sq. ft.
Garage-602 sq. ft.

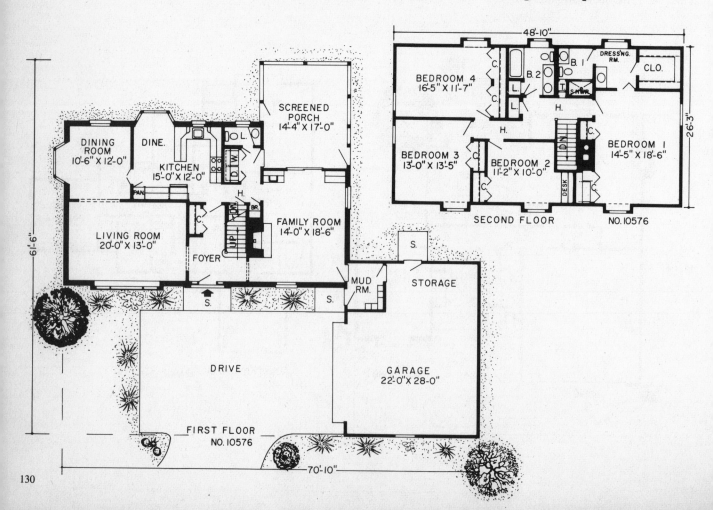

Simple Lines Enhanced By Elegant Window

No. 10503

An arched window in the front den, a sloped ceiling in the living room, and a wall of windows overlooking the rear deck provide a feeling of spaciousness in this elegantly designed home. The dining room opens directly onto the efficiently arranged kitchen. A master suite is appointed with a walk-in closet, double vanities, and a bath.

First floor — 1,486 sq. ft.
Garage — 462 sq. ft.

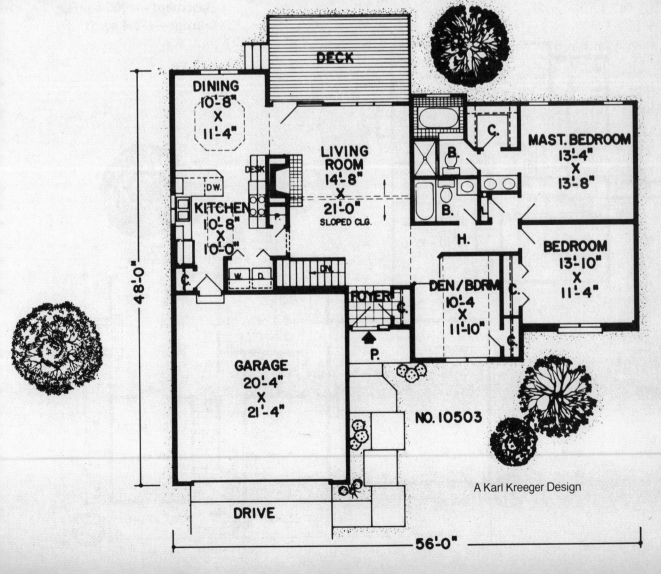

A Karl Kreeger Design

Inviting Porch Enlarges Compact Home

No. 10646

This modified cape with attached two car garage can house a growing family for a bargain price. Double doors in the cozy living room open to the bay-windowed family room with fireplace and patio access. Eat in the family-size kitchen or formal dining room. Up the central stair-way, the vaulted ceiling in the master suite creates a spacious feeling. Three other bedrooms and a bath share the second floor.

First floor — 930 sq. ft.
Second floor — 980 sq. ft
Basement — 900 sq. ft.
Garage — 484 sq. ft.

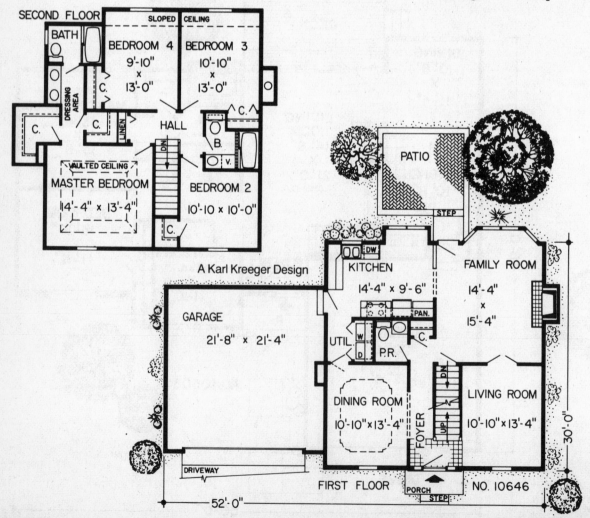

SECOND FLOOR

BATH

DRESSING AREA

SLOPED CEILING

BEDROOM 4
9'-10" x 13'-0"

BEDROOM 3
10'-10" x 13'-0"

C. LINEN

C.

C.

HALL

DN

B.

V.

VAULTED CEILING

MASTER BEDROOM
14'-4" x 13'-4"

BEDROOM 2
10'-10 x 10'-0"

C.

A Karl Kreeger Design

PATIO

STEP

GARAGE
21'-8" x 21'-4"

KITCHEN
14'-4" x 9'-6"

DW

PAN.

FAMILY ROOM
14'-4" x 15'-4"

UTIL

W D

P.R.

C.

DINING ROOM
10'-10"x13'-4"

DN

UP

FOYER

LIVING ROOM
10'-10" x 13'-4"

30'-0"

DRIVEWAY

FIRST FLOOR

PORCH
STEP

NO. 10646

52'-0"

Fireplace Adds Warmth to Family Gatherings

No. 20085

Tudor styling brings a traditional charm to this four-bedroom family home. But, don't expect to sacrifice modern conveniences for a classic look. Living areas surround the spacious central foyer in an efficient plan that links the kitchen with formal and informal dining rooms. Brightened by oversized windows, skylights, and an atrium door to the outdoor deck, the breakfast room is a wonderful place. And, it's just steps away from the elegant, first-floor master suite. Upstairs, everyone has a bedroom, complete with a walk-in closet and a nearby bath.

First floor — 1,806 sq. ft.
Second floor — 883 sq. ft.
Garage — 477 sq. ft.

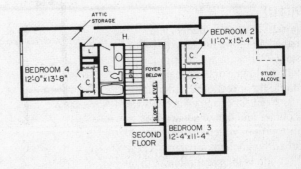

No. 20085

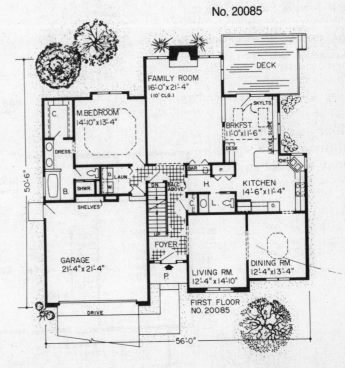

A Karl Kreeger Design

Country Kitchen and Great Room

No. 90419

Front porch, dormers, shutters and multi-paned windows on the exterior of this Cape Cod design are complimented by an informal interior. The main floor is divided into three sections. In the first section is an eat-in country kitchen with island counter and bay window and a large utility room which can be entered from either the kitchen or garage. The second section is the great room with inside fireplace, an informal dining nook and double doors opening onto the rear deck. The master suite features a walk-in closet and compartmentalized bath with linen closet. The upper floor consists of a second full bath and two bedrooms with ample closet space and window seats. A large storage area is provided over the garage.

First floor — 1,318 sq. ft.
Second floor — 718 sq. ft.
Basement — 1,221 sq. ft.
Garage — 436 sq. ft.

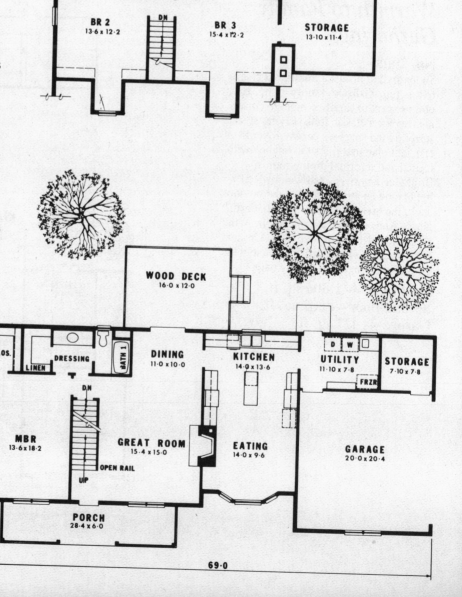

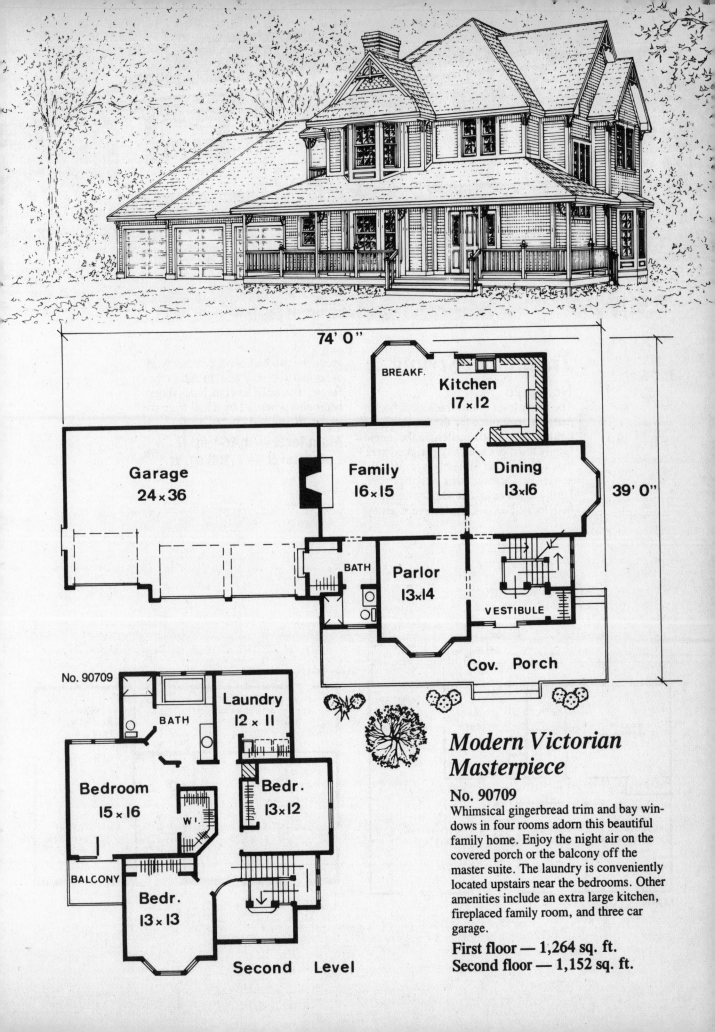

74' 0"

BREAKF.

Kitchen
17 × 12

Garage
24 × 36

Family
16 × 15

Dining
13 × 16

39' 0"

BATH

Parlor
13 × 14

VESTIBULE

Cov. Porch

No. 90709

BATH

Laundry
12 × 11

Bedroom
15 × 16

W.I.

Bedr.
13 × 12

BALCONY

Bedr.
13 × 13

Second Level

Modern Victorian Masterpiece

No. 90709

Whimsical gingerbread trim and bay windows in four rooms adorn this beautiful family home. Enjoy the night air on the covered porch or the balcony off the master suite. The laundry is conveniently located upstairs near the bedrooms. Other amenities include an extra large kitchen, fireplaced family room, and three car garage.

First floor — 1,264 sq. ft.
Second floor — 1,152 sq. ft.

Traditional Styling

No. 90120

The lower level of this traditional home makes a great place for the family to work or play together. Behind the ample family room is a specially designed area that's just perfect for hobbies, crafts, sewing or whatever other activities your family might enjoy. In addition to the bath located on this level, there is also space for two bedrooms or other work areas that you may wish to add in the future. The main level includes three bedrooms separated by a hall from the living, dining and kitchen areas.

Main level — 1,164 sq. ft.
Lower level — 1,108 sq. ft.

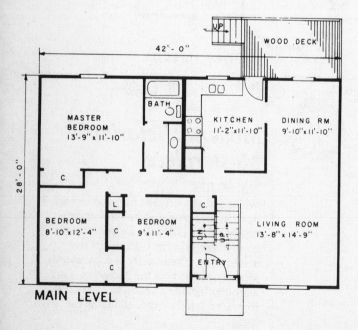

MAIN LEVEL

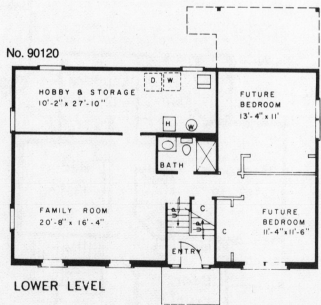

LOWER LEVEL

Semicircular Terrace Offers Access

No. 9882

Spanning four bedrooms to the rear of the home, the semi-circular terrace in this plan is accessible through sliding glass doors from the living room, dining room and family room. The sunken living room with fireplace borders the formal dining room. A kitchen with laundry space is situated to serve both dining room and family room. Three of the bedrooms, including the master bedroom which merits a bath and large closet, face the front and enjoy lovely bay windows.

First floor — 2,212 sq. ft.
Basement — 2,212 sq. ft.
Garage — 491 sq. ft.

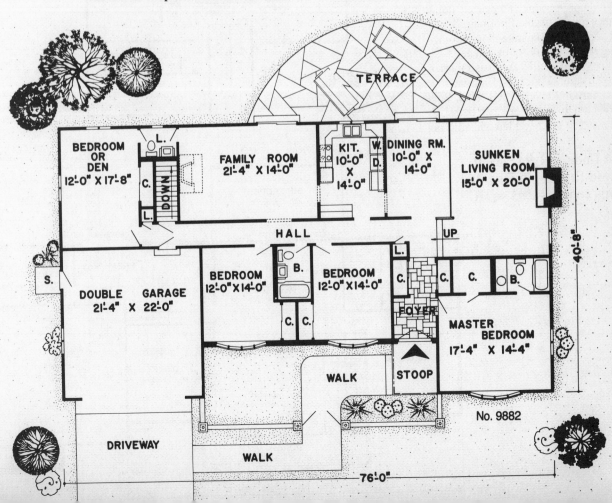

Deluxe Master Suite

No. 90422

Covered porch, stone and painted siding enhance a very livable floor plan. Main level consist of a separate living room, dining room, family room, kitchen, breakfast nook, utility room and master bedroom suite. Upper level consist of three bedrooms and two full baths. Bonus features are three and one-half baths, open stairs in foyer wet bar and attic storage.

First floor — 1,947 sq. ft.
Second floor — 705 sq. ft.
Bonus room — 203 sq. ft.

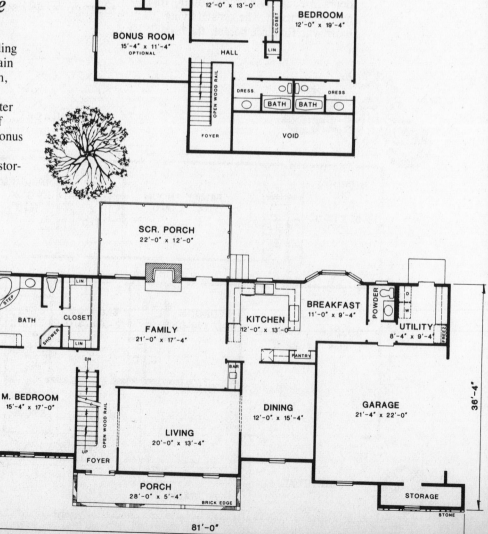

BEDROOM
12'-0" x 13'-0"

BEDROOM
12'-0" x 19'-4"

BONUS ROOM
15'-4" x 11'-4"
OPTIONAL

HALL

CLOSET

CLOSET

LIN

OPEN WOOD RAIL

DRESS

BATH BATH

DRESS

FOYER

VOID

SCR. PORCH
22'-0" x 12'-0"

BATH

CLOSET

LIN

SHOWER

LIN

STEP

FAMILY
21'-0" x 17'-4"

KITCHEN
12'-0" x 13'-0"

BREAKFAST
11'-0" x 9'-4"

POWDER

UTILITY
8'-4" x 9'-4"

FREEZ

DN

BAR

PANTRY

D
W

M. BEDROOM
15'-4" x 17'-0"

OPEN WOOD RAIL

DINING
12'-0" x 15'-4"

GARAGE
21'-4" x 22'-0"

36'-4"

UP

FOYER

STONE

LIVING
20'-0" x 13'-4"

PORCH
28'-0" x 5'-4"

BRICK EDGE

STORAGE

STONE

81'-0"

Eye-appealing Brick Exterior

No. 10559

An elegant Tudor style house design that offers an eye-appealing exterior of brick, stone and stucco masonry. Its airlock foyer leads into a spacious great room with open beam ceilings. Many conveniences are offered in this plan, beginning with all three bedrooms on one floor. Additionally, the master bedroom has a vaulted ceiling plus its own private, very large bath, which comes equipped with both a shower and an oversized tub. Other conveniences include the tasteful connection of the dining, kitchen and pantry rooms. The dining room also has sliding glass doors that lead onto a screened porch for outdoor pleasures. A utility room is located near the two-car garage for added cleanliness of the house.

First floor — 1,809 sq. ft.
Basement — 1,809 sq. ft.
Garage — 585 sq. ft.

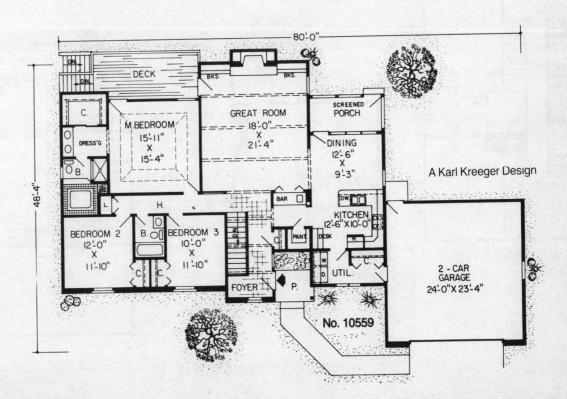

A Karl Kreeger Design

No. 10559

Traditional and Inviting

No. 10575

Warmed by two fireplaces, this classic dutch colonial with central staircase is perfect for a bustling family. With easy access to the back yard, the mudroom is a perfect place for the kids to leave their coats and baseball gloves. Connected by the mudroom, the family room, island kitchen, and breakfast nook feature wood-beamed ceilings. Four bedrooms and two baths upstairs boast ample closet space.

First floor — 1,568 sq. ft.
Second floor — 1,181 sq. ft.
Basement — 1,226 sq. ft.
Garage — 576 sq. ft.

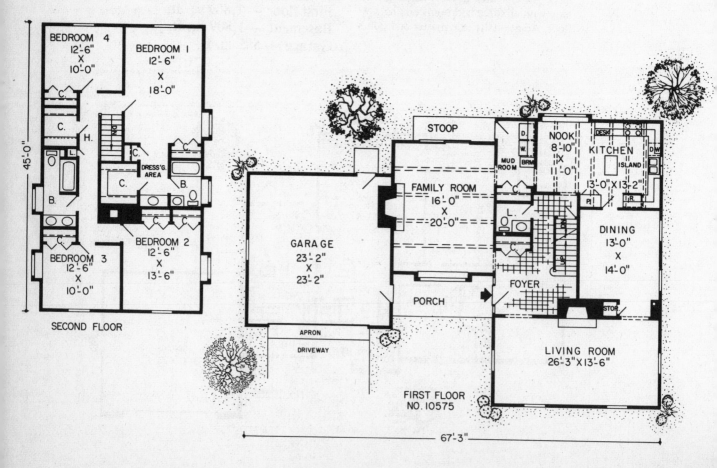

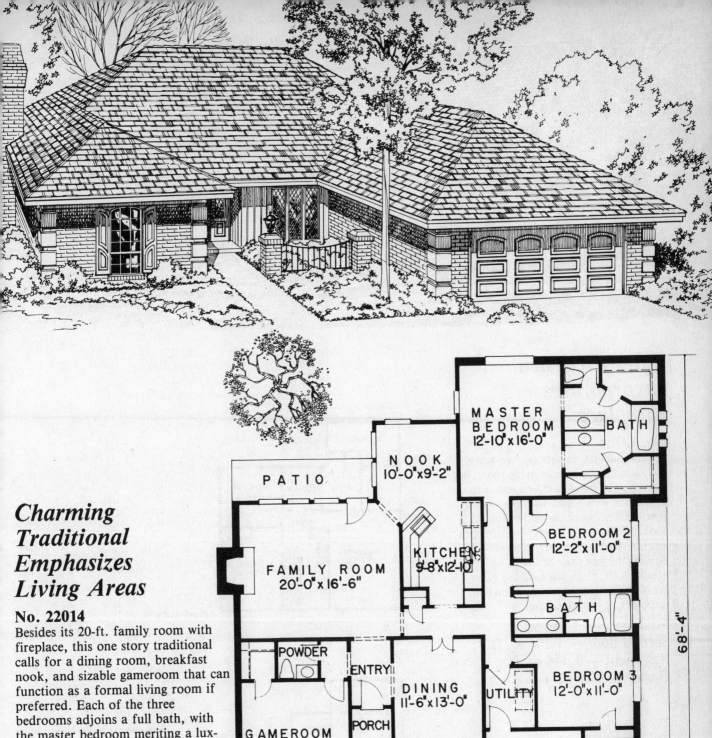

Charming Traditional Emphasizes Living Areas

No. 22014

Besides its 20-ft. family room with fireplace, this one story traditional calls for a dining room, breakfast nook, and sizable gameroom that can function as a formal living room if preferred. Each of the three bedrooms adjoins a full bath, with the master bedroom meriting a luxurious "his and hers" bath with two walk-in closets.

House-2,157 sq. ft.
Garage-485 sq. ft.

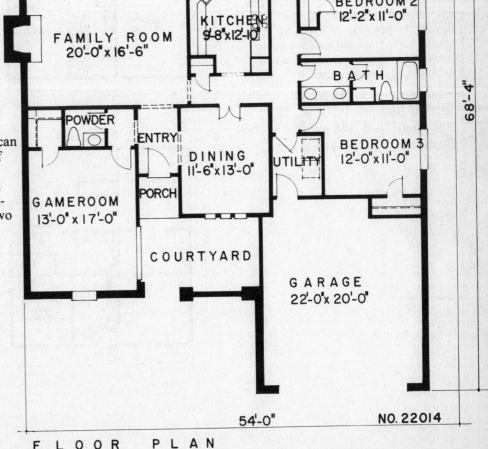

PATIO

NOOK
10'-0" x 9'-2"

MASTER BEDROOM
12'-10" x 16'-0"

BATH

FAMILY ROOM
20'-0" x 16'-6"

KITCHEN
9'-8" x 12'-10"

BEDROOM 2
12'-2" x 11'-0"

BATH

POWDER

ENTRY

DINING
11'-6" x 13'-0"

UTILITY

BEDROOM 3
12'-0" x 11'-0"

PORCH

GAMEROOM
13'-0" x 17'-0"

COURTYARD

GARAGE
22'-0" x 20'-0"

68'-4"

54'-0"

NO. 22014

FLOOR PLAN

Family Kitchen Incorporates Fireplace

No. 19764

For entertaining, this roomy two-story traditional shows a large living room, but for everyday enjoyment, it boasts a family kitchen with corner fireplace, sitting area, built-in bookcase, and a dining nook. Neighboring laundry includes pantry, half-bath, and storage closets. Besides the first floor bedroom with connecting bath, plans call for three generously proportioned bedrooms and two full baths on the upper level.

First floor — 1,586 sq. ft.
Second floor — 1,204 sq. ft.
Basement — 1,346 sq. ft.
Garage — 600 sq. ft.

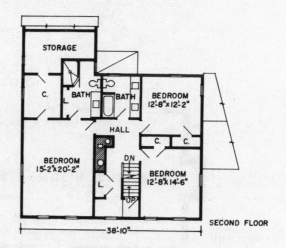

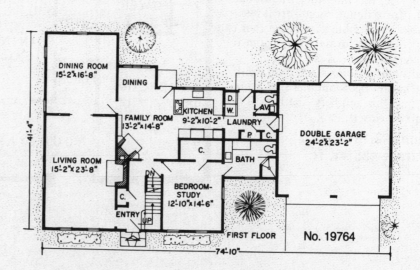

Expandable French Provincial Features Three to Five Bedrooms

No. 90402

This lovely home features a master suite with a deluxe compartmentalized bath which includes a vaulted ceiling with skylights, garden tub, shower, linen closet and a separate dressing room with double vanity and large walk-in closet. Two additional bedrooms with ample closet space share a second compartmentalized bath. Living and dining are lcoated to the side of the formal foyer. A family room with a formal fireplace and double doors on to a screened-in back porch and a U-shaped kitchen with an island counter open to the breakfast bay allow more casual living. Open rail stairs in the family room provide access to the second floor. The second floor can be either unfinished or finished with one or two bedrooms and a large bath.

First floor — 2,400 sq. ft.
Second floor — 751 sq. ft.

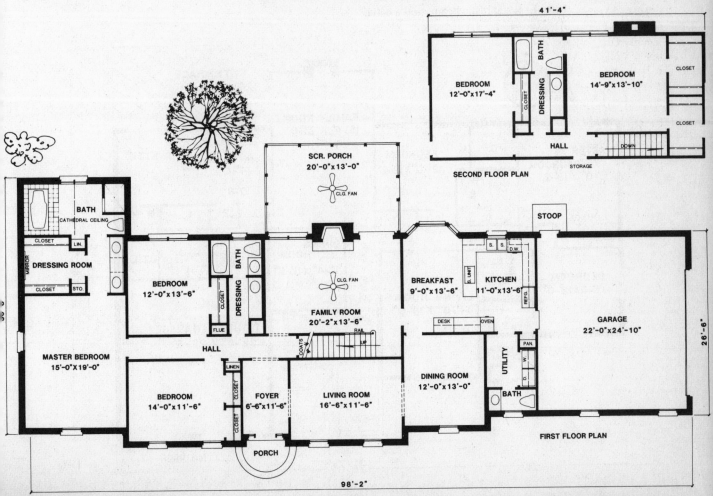

Exterior Promise of Luxury Fulfilled

No. 9998

Graceful Spanish arches and stately brick suggests the right attention to detail that is found inside this expansive three bedroom home. The plush master bedroom suite, a prime example, luxuriates in a lounge, a walk-in closet and a private bath. Exposed rustic beams and a cathedral ceiling heightens the formal living room, and an unusually large family room savors a wood-burning fireplace. In addition to the formal dining room, a kitchen with dinette and access to the terrace is planned.

First floor — 2,333 sq. ft.
Basement — 2,333 sq. ft.
Garage — 559 sq. ft.

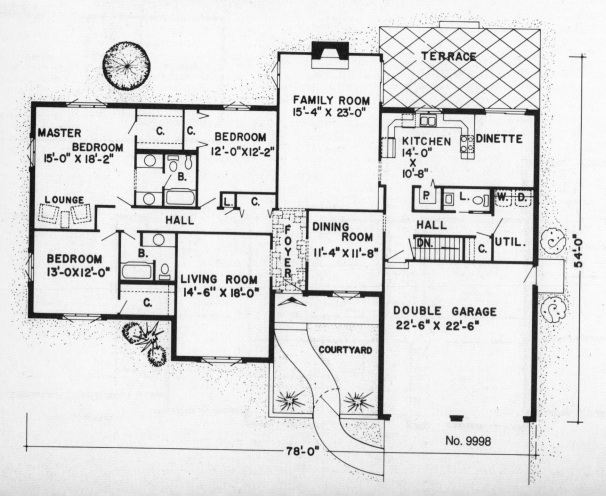

144

Delightful Colonial Design

No. 90138

A quick study of this traditional colonial design will highlight many features desired by homemakers. The exterior of this plan exhibits traditional double-hung windows and horizontal siding all around the house. The first floor living room is completely separated from all other rooms for formal entertaining. The informal family room is at the rear of the house and features a wood-burning fireplace. Sliding glass doors in the breakfast area lead to an outdoor patio which shares its view with the kitchen. A large pantry is located within the kitchen while the laundry facilities are close by. The second floor features four bedrooms and two full baths.

First floor — 1,152 sq. ft.
Second floor — 1,152 sq. ft.

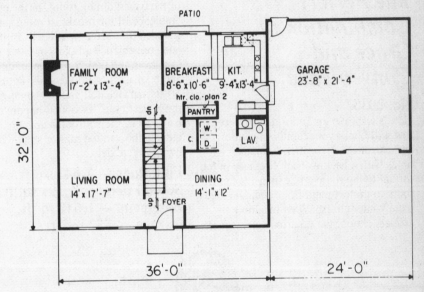

FIRST FLOOR

PLAN 1 WITH BASEMENT
PLAN 2 WITHOUT BASEMENT

No. 90138

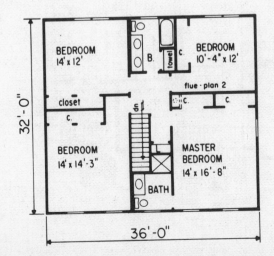

SECOND FLOOR

The Perfect Combination of Grace and Convenience

No. 20352

Here's a sprawling Tudor masterpiece that will house your family in comfort and elegance. An airlock vestibule combines with a back-to-back fireplace in the formal living room and expansive family room to protect main floor common areas from winter chills. When mealtime arrives, choose the luxurious atmosphere of the bayed dining room, or the cheerful ambience of the breakfast room surrounded by a huge, rear deck. Built-ins add convenience and lots of extra storage, from the family room planning desk and bookshelves, to the walk-in pantry off the service hall and the handy bench in the vestibule. Two well-appointed baths serve the bedrooms upstairs, which include the vaulted master suite with its own, private deck.

First floor — 1,647 sq. ft.
Second floor — 1,191 sq. ft.
Basement — 1,647 sq. ft.
Garage — 552 sq. ft.

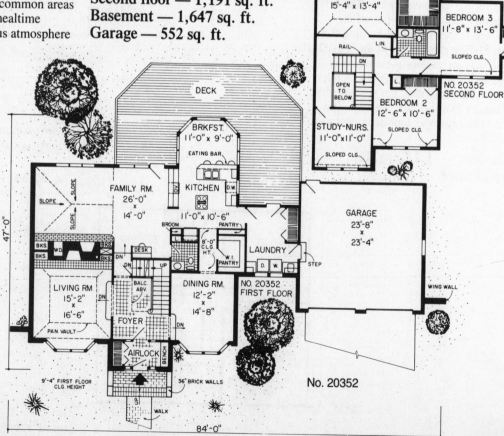

A Design by William E. Gage

Low Maintenance, Southwestern Style

No. 10643

A stucco facade and an arched privacy wall lend a Southwestern flavor to this one-level home with attached garage. Brightened by an open plan and oversized windows, active areas flow together in a convenient, step-saving arrangement. Imagine morning meals in the cheerful kitchen, with the family gathered around the breakfast bar. The adjoining dining room is a perfect spot for a leisurely supper. And, with a brick patio just outside the kitchen door, you can enjoy extra living space in nice weather. Three bedrooms are tucked down a hall for privacy. A huge bay window adds floor space and sunshine to the master suite, which also features its own skylit bath and walk-in closet.

Main living area — 1,285 sq. ft.
Garage — 473 sq. ft.

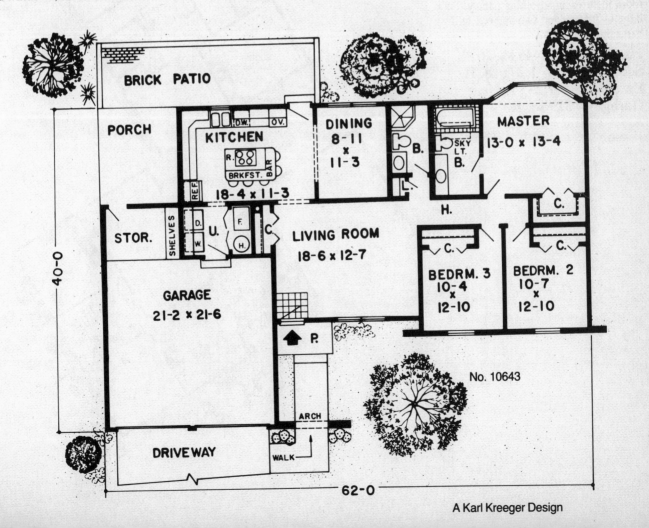

No. 10643

A Karl Kreeger Design

Living Room Favored with Terrace Access

No. 19768

Sliding doors link living room and private terrace in this expansive two story traditional. Also notable are the 14 ft. study with wood-burning fireplace and separate laundry room. The breakfast room features an adjoining pantry. Four large bedrooms and two and one half baths are specified.

First floor — 1,445 sq. ft.
Second floor — 1,271 sq. ft.
Basement — 1,235 sq. ft.
Garage — 529 sq. ft.

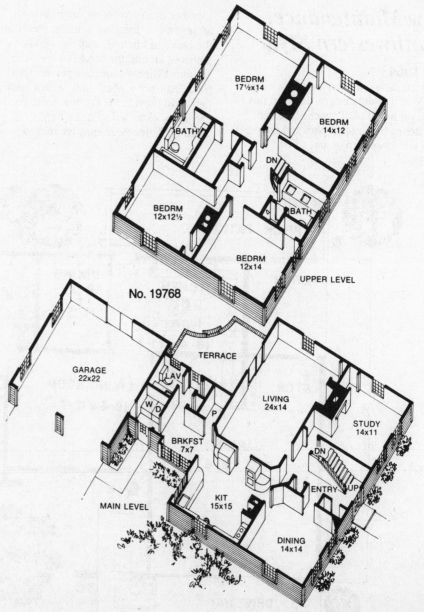

No. 19768

BEDRM 17½x14

BEDRM 14x12

BATH

DN

BATH

BEDRM 12x12½

BEDRM 12x14

UPPER LEVEL

GARAGE 22x22

TERRACE

LAV

W D

P

LIVING 24x14

STUDY 14x11

BRKFST 7x7

DN

ENTRY UP

KIT 15x15

DINING 14x14

MAIN LEVEL

Compact Plan Incorporates Many Amenities

No. 10452

The living and dining rooms join for pleasant family gatherings or entertaining in this well organized plan. More informal activities are centered across the central foyer in the step-saver kitchen and the informal, yet spacious nook with its many windows and built-in hutch. Laundry facilities are located conveniently within the sleeping quarters and near the kitchen area. The large master bedroom with walk-in closets and five piece bath is secluded at the back of the home. The other two bedrooms share an additional bath and each has a roomy closet.

**First floor-1,760 sq. ft.
Garage-433 sq. ft.**

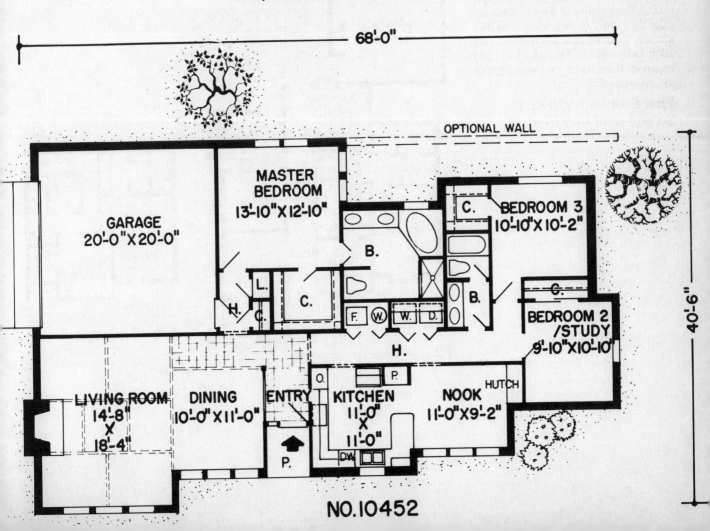

NO. 10452

Focus is on Traditional Style

No. 26840

A quiet comfortable mood is suggested by this traditional design. Public rooms are separated from a secluded master suite and study by a long central gallery which extends to a family room in the rear. A large redwood deck, accessed from the family room and close to the kitchen, guarantees many hours of relaxation and pleasure. Two additional bedrooms and two baths are located above the main floor.

First floor — 1,950 sq. ft.
Second floor — 926 sq. ft.

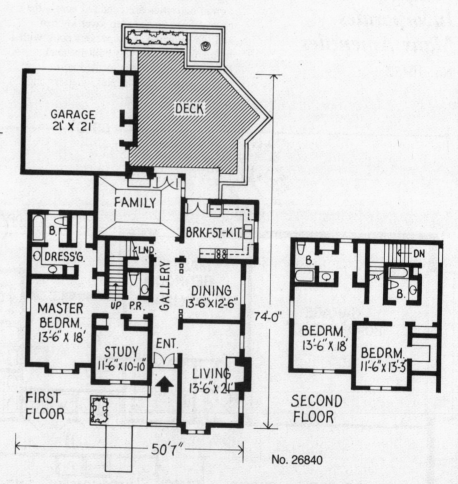

Window Walls Create Garden Atmosphere

No. 10664

Multiple roof lines and twin bay windows give this classic brick home a dramatic exterior that gets even better inside. From the soaring entry to the pool and surrounding patio, active areas are distinctive and exciting. Every room boasts an unusual feature. Look at the two-way bar and fireplace shared by living and family rooms, the built-in hutch and pantry in the dining areas, and the skylit bath in the first-floor master suite. Walk up the U-shaped stairway. You don't often find the luxury of an adjoining bath for each bedroom.

First floor — 2,202 sq. ft.
Second floor — 888 sq. ft.
Garage — 504 sq. ft.

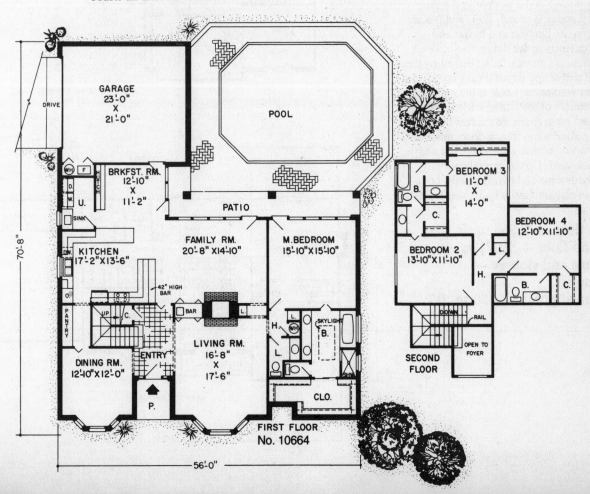

FIRST FLOOR
No. 10664

Master Retreat Crowns Compact Castle

No. 91201

The exterior of this gracious home possesses an elegant air. And inside, built-ins add convenience to every room: stereo storage and a wet bar in the great room; a cooktop island, grill, and baking center in the kitchen; and buffet and china cabinets in the dining room. Even the spacious entrance hall, flanked by the formal parlor and bayed dining room, boasts two closets. Look at the open arrangement of the island kitchen, breakfast, and great rooms at the rear of the house. Sliders and french doors unite this sunny space with a screened porch and the back yard. Up the central stairway, three bedrooms and two full baths complete an elegant family home you'll enjoy for years.

First floor — 1,668 sq. ft.
Second floor — 1,071 sq. ft.
Garage and storage — 580 sq. ft.
Screened porch — 180 sq. ft.

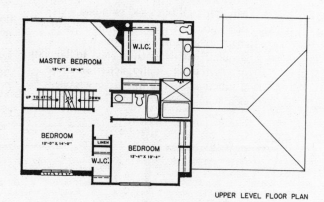

UPPER LEVEL FLOOR PLAN

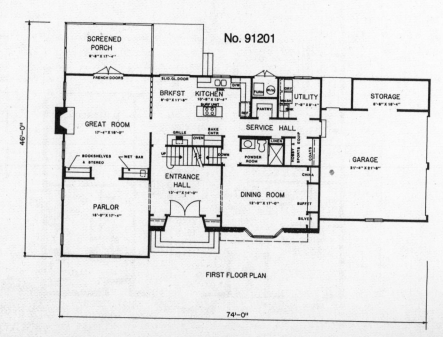

No. 91201

FIRST FLOOR PLAN

Den Offers Peaceful Haven

No. 90923

Here is an exquisite victorian adaptation. The exterior, with its interesting roof lines, window treatment, and inviting entrance porch, could hardly be more dramatic. Inside, the delightfully large, two-story foyer has a beautiful curved staircase and controls the flexible traffic patterns. There's loads of room in this house for formal entertaining. For the family's informal acitvities, family room, covered patio, nook and kitchen areas conveniently interact. Notice the large pantry in the kitchen. Upstairs, via an open balcony hall, you'll find four spacious bedrooms, including the lovely master suite with lavish, sunken tub.

Main floor — 1,264 sq. ft.
Second floor — 1,001 sq. ft.
Unfinished basement —
1,279 sq. ft.
Garage — 456 sq. ft.
Width — 42 ft.
Depth — 56 ft.

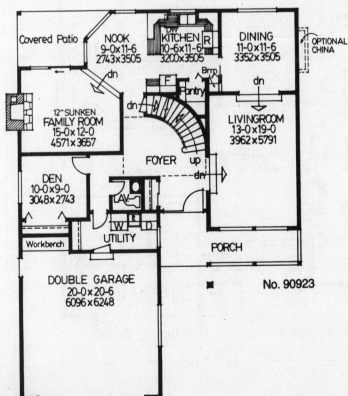

No. 90923

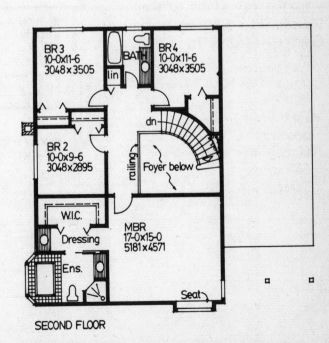

SECOND FLOOR

Leaded Windows Add Sparkle to this Elegant Home

No. 10444

This functional yet elegant floor plan centers on the living room with its 10′ beamed ceiling, fireplace, built-in book-cases and access to the wetbar. A window wall features an inviting view of the patio. The adjacent dining room provides easy access to the efficient yet homey kitchen which features lots of cabinets, a corner sink, a planning desk and a peninsula bar. The bedrooms are grouped at opposite corners of the house. The master suite, complete with fireplace and dressing room, may be adjoined by a convenient den or a fourth bedroom.

First floor — 2,850 sq. ft.
Garage — 462 sq. ft.

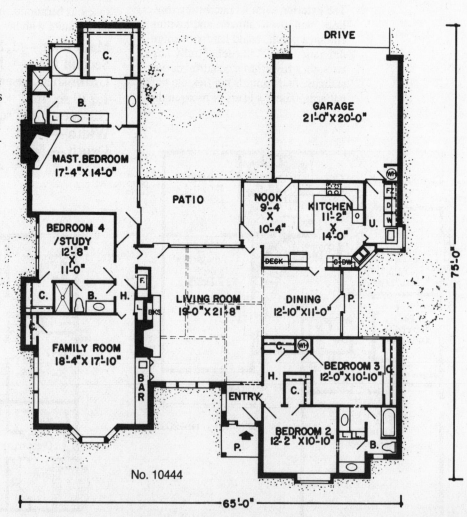

No. 10444

Porch Skirts Stately Traditional

No. 10340

Reminiscent of the past, a functional porch fronts this impressive design and enphasizes the space within. The main level includes formal living and dining rooms, a family room, half bath, utility room, and kitchen with breakfast area and access to the deck. Upstairs are four bedrooms, one with a private bath, another full bath with double vanity, and an abundance of closets.

First floor — 1,212 sq. ft.
Second floor — 1,210 sq. ft.
Basement — 1,210 sq. ft.
Garage — 576 sq. ft.
Breezeway — 115 sq. ft.

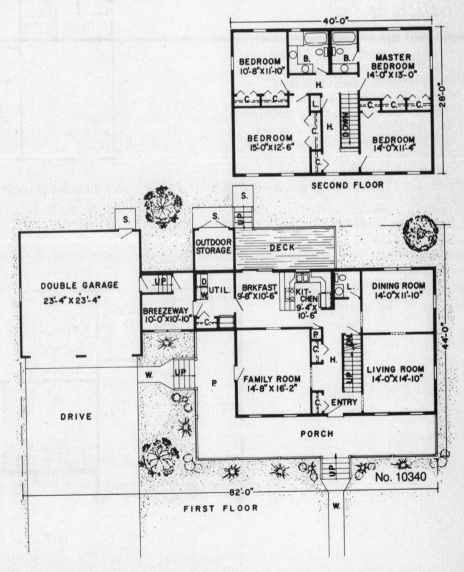

Elegant Yet Energy Efficient

No. 90110

From the central foyer, the staircase rises to the elegantly arranged bedrooms. The master bedroom features a dressing room, master bath and walk-in closet. The other bedrooms are convenient to the other upstairs bath with its double lavatory. The first floor encompasses several distinct living areas, including a family room with fireplace, a formal dining room, and a kitchen with its own dining area.

First floor — 1,398 sq. ft.
Second floor — 1,266 sq. ft.

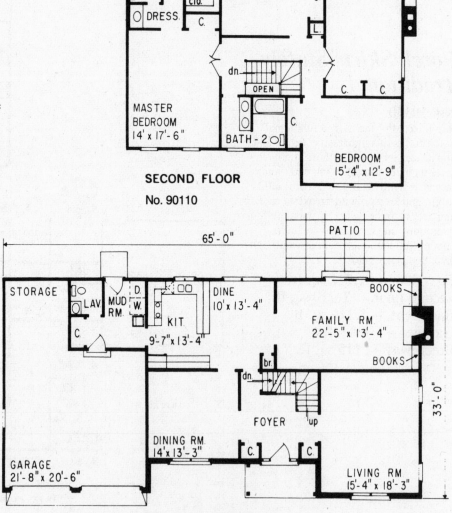

SECOND FLOOR

No. 90110

FIRST FLOOR

Master Bedroom on First Level

No. 90142

This excellent traditional design has the master bedroom located on the first level and equipped with a walk-in closet and a large bath area that incorporates a skylight over the tub. Also on the first level is a living room with large bay windows allowing natural lighting to fill the room. The kitchen has an abundance of cabinet space and includes a pantry that has plenty of storage space. The laundry room is located just between the kitchen and garage. The second level has three bedrooms and one full bath.

First floor — 1,663 sq. ft.
Second floor — 727 sq. ft.

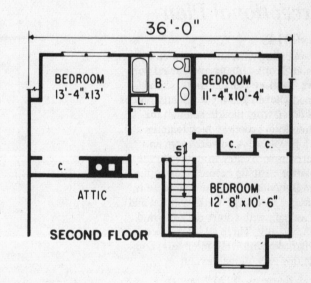

36'-0"

BEDROOM
13'-4" x 13'

B.
L.

BEDROOM
11'-4" x 10'-4"

c.

c.   c.

ATTIC

BEDROOM
12'-8" x 10'-6"

SECOND FLOOR

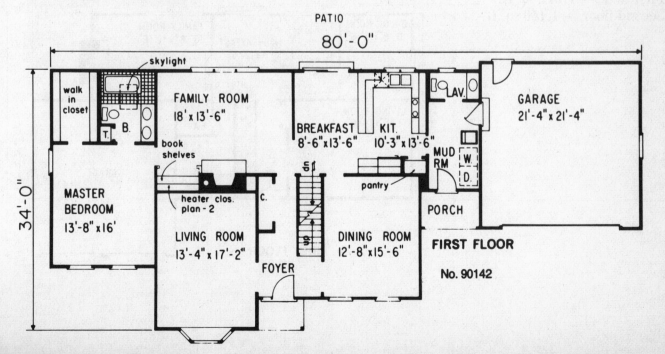

PATIO

80'-0"

skylight

walk in closet

FAMILY ROOM
18' x 13'-6"

BREAKFAST
8'-6" x 13'-6"

KIT.
10'-3" x 13'-6"

LAV.

GARAGE
21'-4" x 21'-4"

T.   B.

book shelves

heater clos.
plan - 2

c.

pantry

MUD RM

W.   D.

34'-0"

MASTER BEDROOM
13'-8" x 16'

LIVING ROOM
13'-4" x 17'-2"

DINING ROOM
12'-8" x 15'-6"

PORCH

FOYER

FIRST FLOOR

No. 90142

Classic Styling, Exceptional Plan

No. 90155

An appealing exterior is accented by the second floor overhang and gabled windows. A snack counter divides the U-shaped kitchen and breakfast area. Steps lead down from the kitchen into the sunken living room, which features a brick fireplace. A powder room and mudroom with entry from the garage allow for clean up before entering the main living areas. The master suite is enhanced by a large walk-in closet and deluxe bath with corner deck tub and double vanity. Three additional bedrooms, two with walk-in closets, complete this exceptional layout.

First floor — 1,212 sq. ft.
Second floor — 1,160 sq. ft.

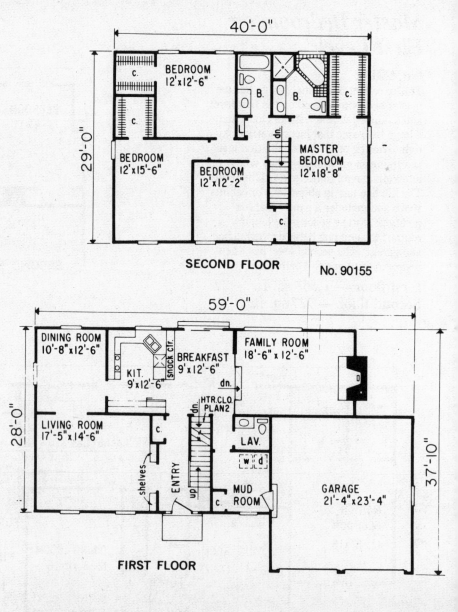

SECOND FLOOR   No. 90155

FIRST FLOOR

Country Comfort

No. 91204

Imagine back yard barbecues on the rear deck off this rambling ranch house. The handy kitchen pass-through will insure that serving the side dishes will be a simple matter. You'll love the convenience of the eat-in country kitchen off the foyer. Want a formal atmosphere? Close off the bustle of mealtime preparation with sliding panels. And, after supper, put up your feet, sit by the fire and enjoy the airy atmosphere that soaring ceilings and sliding glass doors give the sunken great room. Three bedrooms are tucked away from active areas. Look at the master suite. Even the largest wardrobe will fit in those twin walk-in closets!

**Main living area — 1,974 sq. ft.
Garage and storage —
612 sq. ft.**

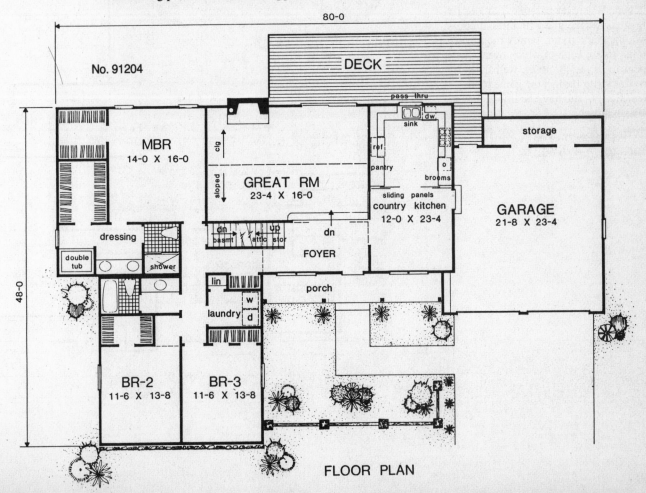

FLOOR PLAN

One Level Home Offers Utility Room, Pantry

No. 22000

Inside its gracious hip roof exterior, this single level plan shows well-defined living areas and such extras as a utility room off the garage and a pantry off the kitchen. Wherever possible, outdoor living areas are merged with those indoors, as in the game room, family room and dining room, each of which overlooks or opens to patios. A closet, wetbar, and powder room furnish the game room area. Each of the three bedrooms has a walk-in closet.

Living area — 2,094 sq. ft.
Garage — 498 sq. ft.

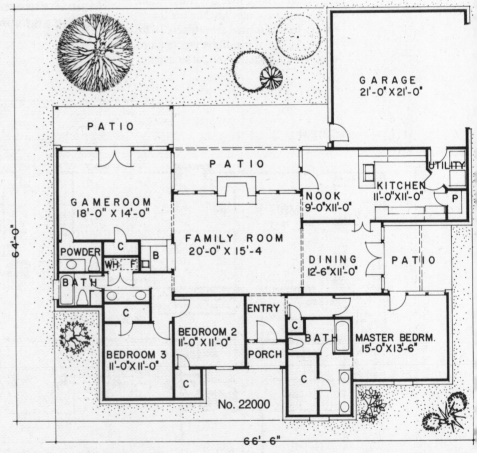

Light, Airy, and Easy-Care

No. 91218

Here's a convenient plan with a wide-open feeling. Walk up the stairs from the foyer and survey the spacious, two-story living room below, heated by a massive fireplace that will warm the whole house. Convenient features upstairs include double sinks in the skylit master bath, a handy chute that delivers dirty clothes right to the laundry facilities, and a full bath and dressing room adjoining the other bedrooms. Downstairs, you'll marvel at the step-saving layout of the island kitchen that serves the formal dining room, breakfast room, and screened porch with ease.

First floor — 945 sq. ft.
Second floor — 1,108 sq. ft.
Screened porch — 106 sq. ft.
Garage — 484 sq. ft.

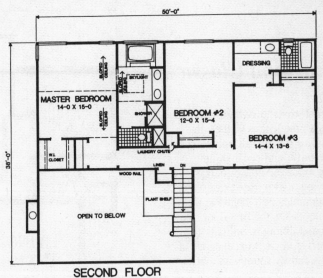

SECOND FLOOR

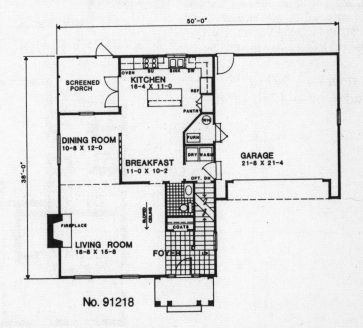

No. 91218

New England Classic

No. 26850

This updated 18th century traditional home offers a practical as well as an attractive choice for today's homeowner. The wood exterior and cedar shingle roofing help make the house energy-efficient. Wood is also used extensively throughout the interior to continue the traditional mood. On the first floor, the living room and dining room flank a large foyer offering an immediate air of hospitality. A family room with a brick hearth, a kitchen with a center work island, and a bedroom suite are also featured. Upstairs there are three additional bedrooms and a laundry room. The master suite has a fireplace and a private bath.

First floor — 1,297 sq. ft.
Second floor — 1,091 sq. ft.

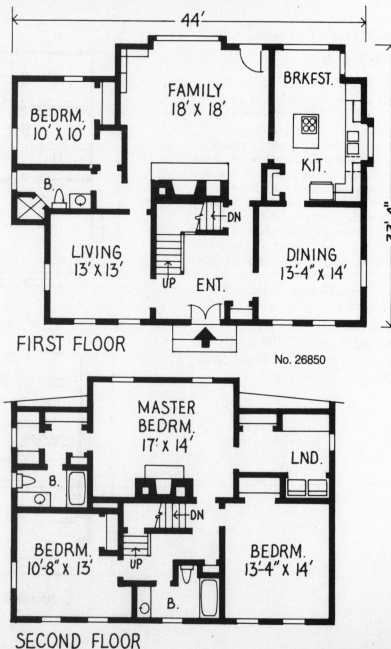

Design Calls for Formal Living Areas

No. 19718

Shuttered, small-paned windows accent a traditional exterior, while on the inside, formal living and dining rooms balance this paneled informality of the family room. For convenience, the kitchen borders a breakfast room and extra large utility room with space for laundry equipment and freezer. Featured is the private study with built-in bookshelves.

Living area — 2,421 sq. ft.
Garage — 560 sq. ft.

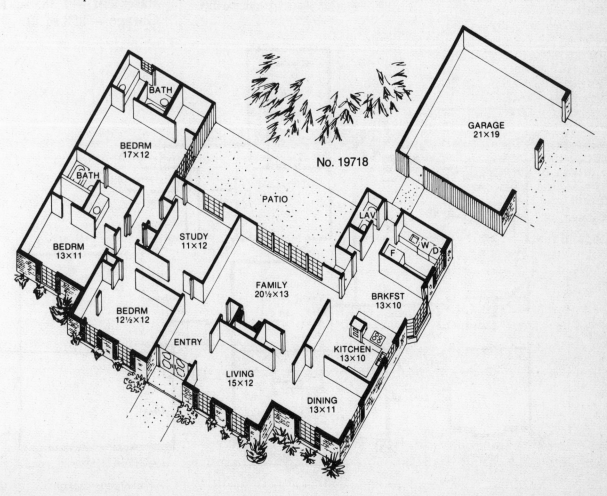

No. 19718

GARAGE
21×19

BATH

BEDRM
17×12

BATH

PATIO

LAV

W D

F

BEDRM
13×11

STUDY
11×12

FAMILY
20½×13

BRKFST
13×10

BEDRM
12½×12

ENTRY

KITCHEN
13×10

LIVING
15×12

DINING
13×11

Get Ready for Exciting Interior Views

No. 10545

You'll find all the common living areas on the foyer level of this intriguing home. A formal dining room just off the entry enjoys a sun-filled atmosphere, thanks to floor-to-ceiling windows overlooking the front yard. Past the powder room and laundry, an island kitchen features a planning desk, a built-in bar that serves the spacious great room, and a skylit sun room just perfect for morning coffee or informal family meals. The rear deck will double your warm-weather living space. Six stairs up from the foyer, off a curved hallway, two bedrooms and two full baths include the high-ceilinged master suite with its cozy sitting area. An open loft at the top of the house leads to two more bedrooms and an adjoining full bath.

Main levels — 2,162 sq. ft.
Upper level — 722 sq. ft.
Basement — 1,385 sq. ft.
Garage — 858 sq. ft.

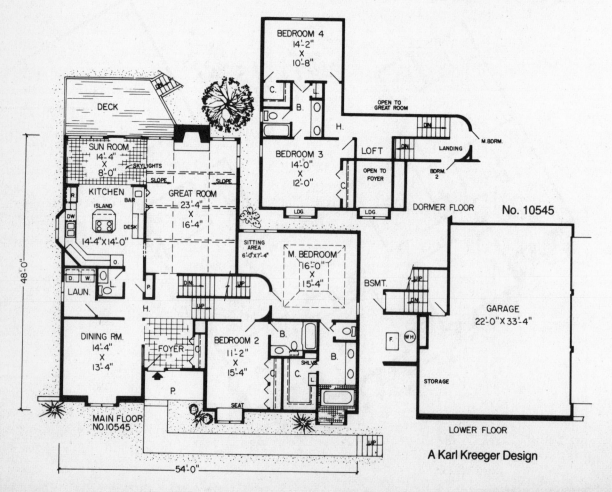

A Karl Kreeger Design

164

Raised Tub Fills Bump-Out Window

No. 91220

A sturdy stucco exterior, adorned by graceful arches and a curved stair rail, hints at the gracious touches inside this elegant home. On the garage level, you'll find the huge play room, game room, adjoining outdoor patio, powder room, and laundry facilities. Upstairs, above the front entry level, you'll find the active areas of the house. The high-ceilinged living room features a cozy fireplace and shares access to the rear deck with the master suite around the corner. Formal dining and breakfast rooms flank the efficient island kitchen, insuring step-saving meal preparation. Two bedrooms off the foyer share a full bath.

Upper level — 2,060 sq. ft.
Lower level — 1,045 sq. ft.
Garage — 536 sq. ft.

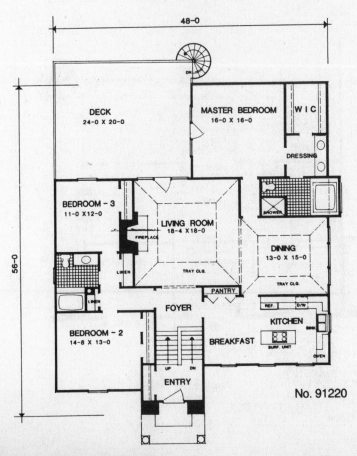

No. 91220

UPPER LEVEL FLOOR PLAN

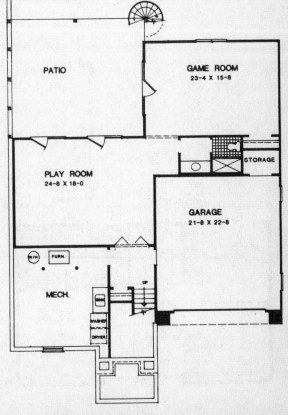

LOWER LEVEL FLOOR PLAN

Tudor Grandeur for the Budget-Minded

No. 20354

Gracious living is within your reach if you choose this updated, three-bedroom Tudor. Distinguished by an elegant, centuries-old facade of stucco, brick, and multi-pane transom windows, and a plan that uses every inch of space, this home affords its owners all the amenities of a larger house. A two-story foyer divides the main floor into formal and family areas. Notice the built-ins throughout: window seats in the living and dining rooms, the convenient range-top island and planters that separate the expansive family areas, and the handy bar tucked into a corner of the sun room off the breakfast nook. Your houseplant collection on the ledge above the stairwell will add a greenhouse feeling to the second floor hall that links the spacious bedrooms and two well-appointed baths.

First floor — 1,346 sq. ft.
Second floor — 1,196 sq. ft.
Basement — 1,346 sq. ft.
Garage — 840 sq. ft.

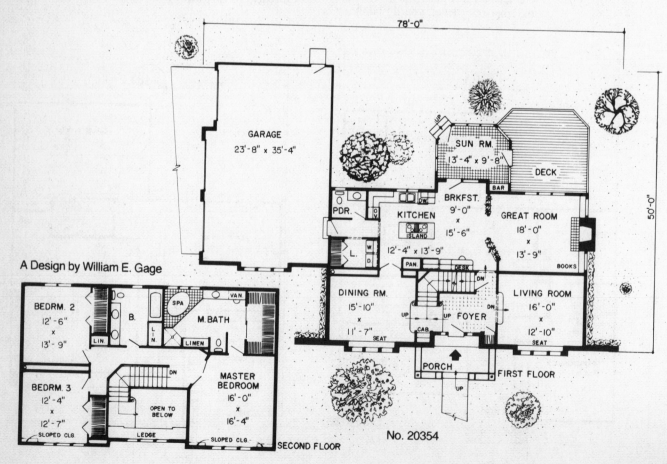

A Design by William E. Gage

No. 20354

SECOND FLOOR

FIRST FLOOR

Lead Glass Enhances Arched Window Treatment

No. 10460

Multiple arched windows spill light into every corner of this handsome design. The beamed ceiling of the living room plus its wetbar, bookshelves and fireplace invite gracious living. The adjacent covered patio is illuminated by skylights and opens onto the family room. The large master suite features a five-piece bath with a curved glass wall plus a four-wall walk-in closet. The other two bedrooms share a walk-through bath.

First floor — 2,497 sq. ft.
Garage — 496 sq. ft.

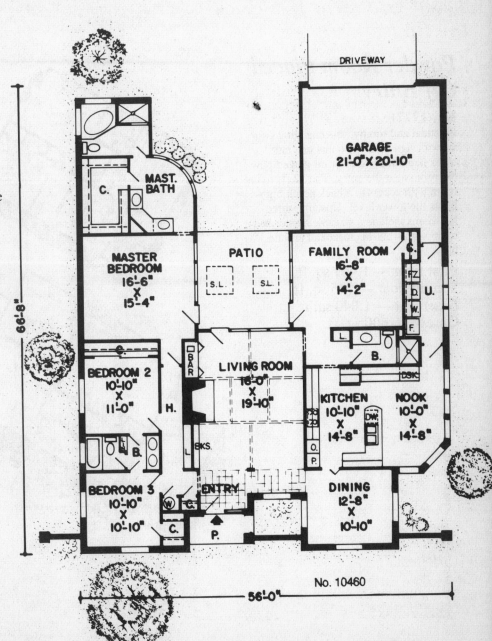

No. 10460

Powder Room Placed Off Entry

No. 19771

Practical and roomy, this engaging two story design offers two and one half baths in addition to the well-placed powder room near the entry. The 32 ft. living room with access to a back porch highlights the lower level. Upstairs, three bedrooms include a sizeable master bedroom with walk-in closet and private bath.

First floor — 1,409 sq. ft.
Second floor — 915 sq. ft.
Basement — 1,040 sq. ft.
Garage — 600 sq. ft.

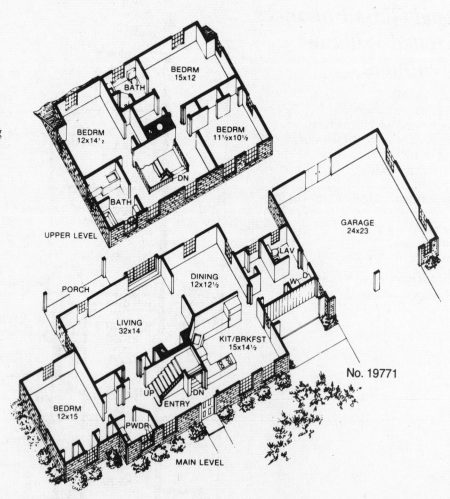

Skylit Loft Crowns
Updated Traditional

No. 10754

Touches of old and new unite to make this a perfect home for the modern family. Rough-hewn beams adorn 11-foot ceilings in the fireplaced living room, mirroring the classic Tudor exterior. Elegant, recessed ceilings grace the master suite and formal dining room. Energy-saving fans lend an old-fashioned air to these lovely rooms. But, the modern plan brings efficiency to the huge island kitchen, which serves the dining room, breakfast nook, and adjacent deck with ease. And, the first-floor master suite, with its double vanities, walk-in closets, and luxurious whirlpool tub, is a convenient feature you're sure to appreciate. Tucked upstairs, two additional bedrooms adjoin a full bath.

First floor — 1,962 sq. ft.
Second floor — 870 sq. ft.
Garage — 611 sq. ft.

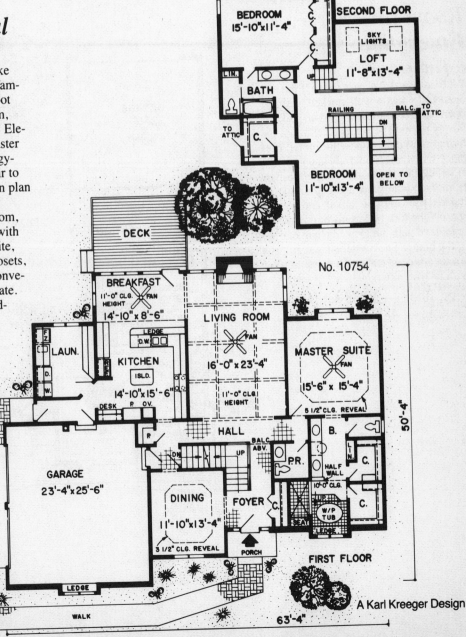

A Karl Kreeger Design

Glass-walled Family Room Invites Entertaining

No. 10466

With convenient access through the breakfast nook, a well-stocked wetbar opens into both the living room and the family room. The beamed ceiling of the living room plus its hearth-rimmed fireplace will appeal to family and guests alike. The kitchen sink is bathed in light from the corner greenhouse windows and flanked by plenty of cabinet and counter space. The four bedrooms of this well-organized plan are located along one wall of the home. The master suite features a corner window-seat and a dressing room with its own skylight.

First floor — 2,285 sq. ft.
Garage — 483 sq. ft.

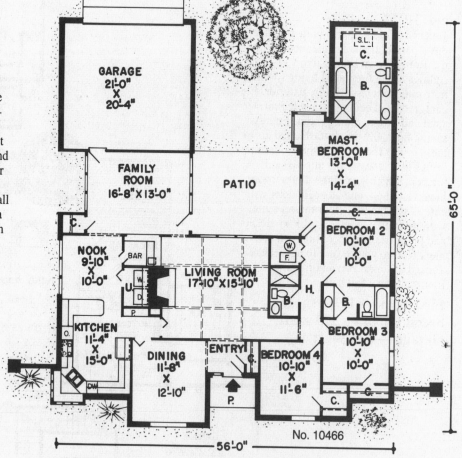

GARAGE 21'-0" X 20'-4"

FAMILY ROOM 16'-8" X 13'-0"

PATIO

MAST. BEDROOM 13'-0" X 14'-4"

BEDROOM 2 10'-10" X 10'-0"

NOOK 9'-10" X 10'-0"

BAR

LIVING ROOM 17'-10" X 15'-10"

KITCHEN 11'-4" X 15'-0"

DINING 11'-6" X 12'-10"

ENTRY

BEDROOM 4 10'-10" X 11'-6"

BEDROOM 3 10'-10" X 10'-0"

65'-0"

56'-0"

No. 10466

Plan Sports Solar Room with Hot Tub

No. 10384

English Tudor styling and a two-story passive solar room with a hot tub are appealing features of the design you see here. 8″ brick walls and a 6″ concrete floor in the solar room soak up heat during the day and slowly release the warmth at night. Sliding glass doors and windows next to the solar room in a bath, kitchen and dining area on the lower level and two bedrooms on the upper level, can be opened or closed to control warm air circulation from the solar room. Also found on the lower level are a den and a sunken living room. Two bedrooms and a large master suite are located on the upper level. Balconies look onto the solar room below from two of the bedrooms, incluing the master bedroom. A double garage and shop, three baths and ample storage finish the floor plan. Simulated stucco or stucco panels finish the exterior appeal.

First floor — 964 sq. ft.
Second floor — 864 sq. ft.
Basement — 964 sq. ft.
Garage — 678 sq. ft.
Solar room — 272 sq. ft.

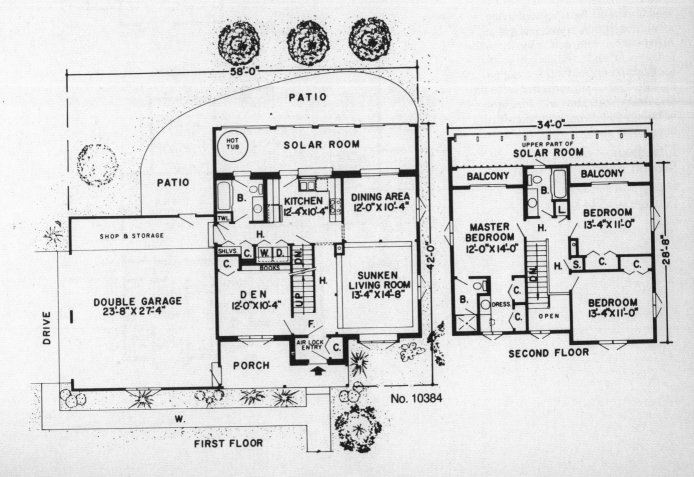

You Deserve this Classic Beauty

No. 20094

Sturdy stucco, fieldstone, and rough-hewn timbers lend a distinguished air to this updated Tudor classic. And inside, modern and traditional elements unite to create a masterpiece your family will never outgrow. Look at the soaring foyer, the elegant recessed ceilings in the dining room and master suite, and the book-lined library off the fireplaced living room. Imagine the convenience of an island kitchen with wetbar service to the living room, and an adjoining, skylit breakfast room. And, think about how the three-and-a-half baths that serve the first-floor master suite and three upstairs bedrooms will make the morning rush a thing of the past.

First floor — 2,047 sq. ft.
Second floor — 789 sq. ft.
Basement — 2,047 sq. ft.
Garage — 524 sq. ft.

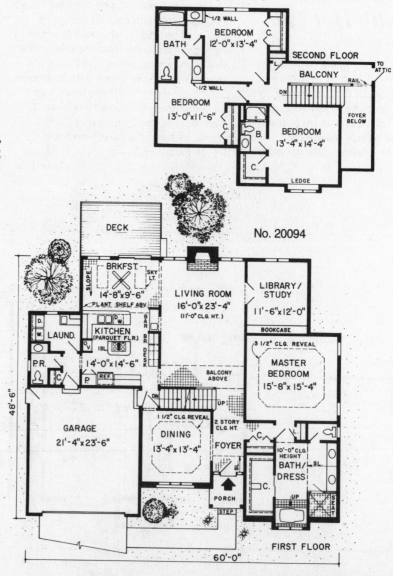

A Karl Kreeger Design

Traditional Warmth with a Modern Accent

No. 10638

Gracious touches make this spacious dwelling a place you'll love to come home to. Look at the recessed ceilings in the living, dining, and master bedrooms. Rustic beams, a cozy fireplace, and built-in shelves make the family room special. Notice the efficient placement of kitchen and utility areas adjacent to formal and informal dining rooms. With four bedrooms upstairs, this is a perfect family home. You can watch the kids playing on the patio from the cozy bay-windowed sitting nook in the master suite.

First floor — 1,405 sq. ft.
Second floor — 1,364 sq. ft.
Garage — 458 sq. ft.

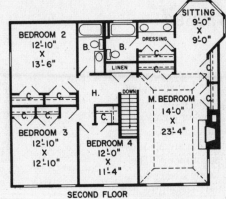

SECOND FLOOR

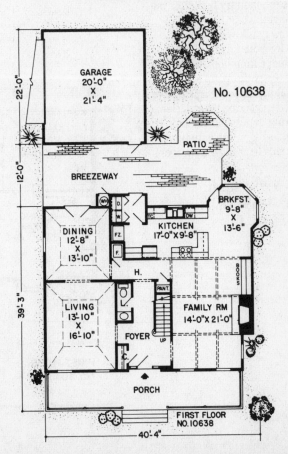

No. 10638

FIRST FLOOR
NO. 10638

Exterior Exposed Beams

No. 10437

40 inch high bookshelves line several of the family and living room walls, giving the reader or family collector plenty of space to display his treasures. Patio access, a fireplace and a bar are also featured in these two adjacent rooms. The central portion of the home is very functional and work oriented. The utility area not only houses the laundry facilities, but also the furnace and water heater. Hallways and a stairway allow for smooth traffic patterns for both levels. The kitchen and casual eating nook to the rear share a view of the patio, patio access and abundant cabinet space. Pleasing eye appeal and variety describe the exterior facade. Interesting details include bay windows, false dormers, brick quoins and exposed beams near the dining room and entry.

First floor— 1,954 sq. ft.
Second floor — 685 sq. ft.
Garage — 556 sq. ft.

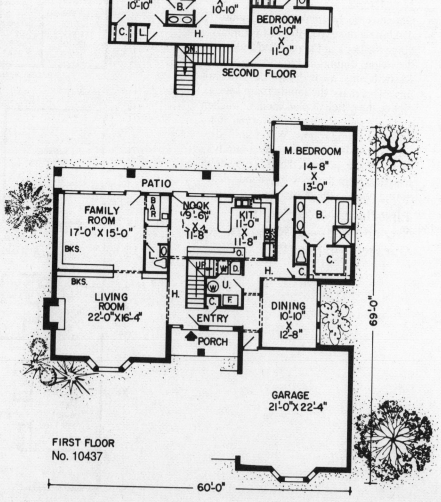

Family-Preferred Features in Tudor Design

No. 10568

Many family-preferred features are offered in this deluxe Tudor design. An energy efficient foyer leads into a great room that has its own wood-burning fireplace. Off of the great room lies the master bedroom, the only bedroom on the first level. The master bedroom has its own private wood deck, and the bath area has a two way shower and a his/her bathroom space with separate facilities. Also on the first level is an efficient kitchen with a large breakfast nook, and just off the kitchen is a utility room. The second level includes a cedar closet, a loft area that overlooks the great room below and two bedrooms that share a full bath.

First floor — 2,167 sq.ft.
Second floor — 755 sq.ft.
Basement — 2,224 sq.ft.
Garage — 1,020 sq.ft.

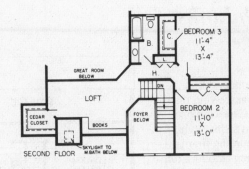

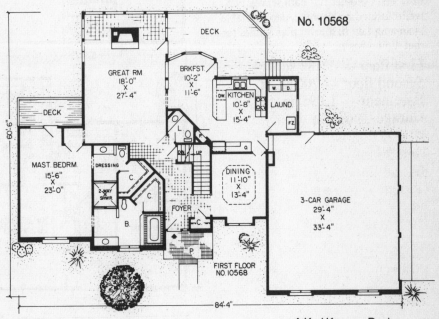

A Karl Kreeger Design

Roofed Porch Links Home, Garage

No. 19761

Located to encourage outdoor dining, a sizable porch links the garage with the kitchen complex of this Cape Cod plan. Off the entrance hall, the formal living room provides a wood-burning fireplace, and the first floor bedroom adjoins a full bath with linen closet, vanity, and walk-in closet. Another full bath serves two well-closeted bedrooms. Also available is an alternate first level plan with a formal dining room.

First floor — 1,187 sq. ft.
Second floor — 700 sq. ft.
Basement — 1,095 sq. ft.
Garage — 675 sq. ft.

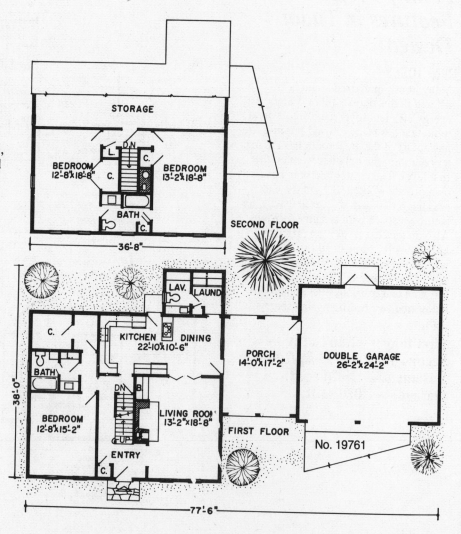

Tudor Romance

No. 10743

Cramped for space? Here's a classic family home with lots of room, and plenty of style. The central foyer reveals a U-shaped staircase that leads to four bedrooms and two full baths. Notice the elegant master suite, with its recessed ceilings, private deck, and abundant closet space. French doors add a romantic flair to the formal dining room, study, and glass-walled sunroom. The kitchen, dinette, and fireplaced family room wrap around the central staircase for an open feeling. Look at the huge pantry tucked under the stairs, and the efficient cooktop island in the kitchen. On lazy summer days, you'll love basking in the sun on the deck off the family room.

First floor — 1,466 sq. ft.
Second floor — 1,106 sq. ft.
Garage — 589 sq. ft.

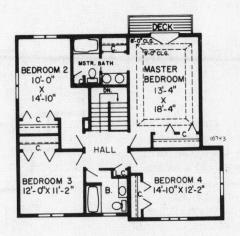

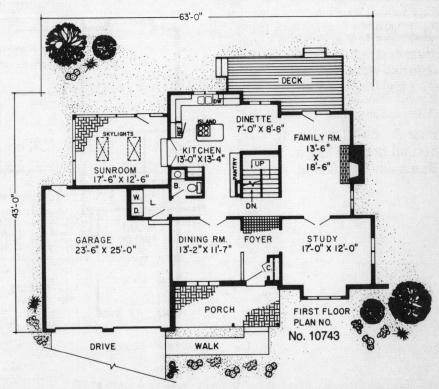

175

Family Living on Two Levels

No. 20090

Stacked window towers grace the facade of this spacious, four-bedroom classic with attached garage. The formal parlor and dining room right off the foyer feature decorative ceilings. Family areas at the rear of the house are arranged for convenient access to the island kitchen. You'll love the skylit breakfast room with its surrounding outdoor deck. And, when there's a chill in the air, you'll appreciate the coziness of a fireplace in the family room. Send the kids upstairs at bedtime, where three bedrooms share a roomy, skylit bath with double vanities. You can enjoy your first-floor master suite that includes double vanities, a huge, walk-in closet, and an elegant recessed ceiling.

First floor — 1,888 sq. ft.
Second floor — 833 sq. ft.
Basement — 1,888 sq. ft.

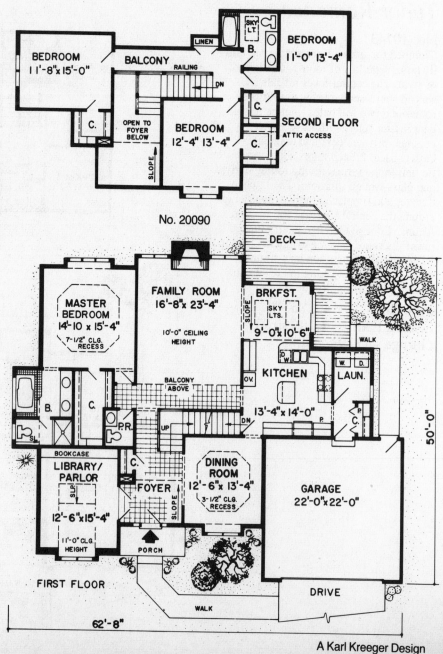

No. 20090

SECOND FLOOR

BEDROOM 11'-8"x15'-0"
BALCONY
RAILING
LINEN
B.
BEDROOM 11'-0" 13'-4"
C.
OPEN TO FOYER BELOW
DN
BEDROOM 12'-4" 13'-4"
C.
C.
ATTIC ACCESS
SLOPE

FIRST FLOOR

DECK
MASTER BEDROOM 14'-10 x 15'-4"
7-1/2" CLG. RECESS
FAMILY ROOM 16'-8"x 23'-4"
10'-0" CEILING HEIGHT
BRKFST. 9'-0"x10'-6"
SKY LTS.
SLOPE
WALK
B.
C.
KITCHEN 13'-4"x 14'-0"
LAUN.
W. D.
OV.
BALCONY ABOVE
PR.
UP
DN
P.
C.
BOOKCASE
LIBRARY/ PARLOR 12'-6"x15'-4"
11'-0" CLG HEIGHT
C.
FOYER
SLOPE
DINING ROOM 12'-6"x 13'-4"
3-1/2" CLG. RECESS
GARAGE 22'-0"x22'-0"
50'-0"
PORCH
WALK
62'-8"
DRIVE

A Karl Kreeger Design

178

Secret Room Incorporated into this Luxury Home Plan

No. 10458

Hidden in the recesses of the master bedroom's walk-in closet is a secret room for valuables. The remainder of the master closet has built-in dressers, and a skylight illuminates the adjoining five-piece bath. The centrally located living room is accented by beamed, 10-foot ceilings plus bookcases and a fireplace. The large, yet efficient kitchen conveniently divides the formal dining room from the more informal nook which looks onto the patio. The family room, complete with wetbar and its own fireplace is located at the rear of the house and has a wall of windows overlooking the lawn.

First floor — 2,925 sq.ft.
Garage — 490 sq.ft.

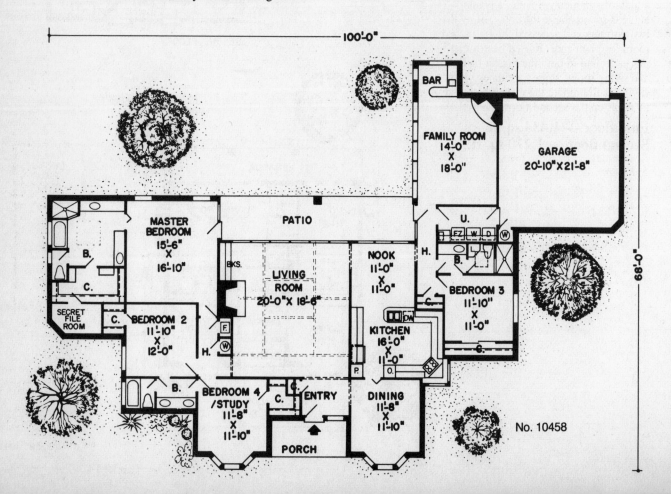

No. 10458

Attractive Entry Created by Plant Ledge

No. 10438

Dormers, decorative gable vents, and bay windows balance on either side of the front entrance to give the exterior facade a look of symmetry. Inside, a planter ledge is found above the entry, lit by the two dormers and accessed through a bedroom for plant care. Raised hearth fireplaces, found in both the master bedroom and living room, share a chimney. Two skylights illuminate the master bath and all areas on the second floor.

First floor — 1,454 sq. ft.
Second floor — 1,270 sq. ft.

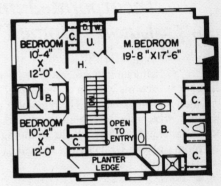

SECOND FLOOR

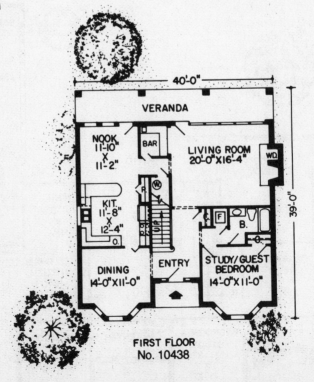

FIRST FLOOR
No. 10438

Rough Siding and Brick Grace Ranch Style

No. 9364

Its low silhouette punctuated by rough vertical siding and red brick, this three bedroom ranch style presents a singularly striking facade. Entry is via the long cov-ered porch and into the closeted foyer, with the living room at the right. To the rear, the family room and kitchen cooper-ate in creating a complex for living, working and eating that combines laun-dry niche, pantry and sliding glass doors to the patio. The master bedroom enjoys double closets and a full bath, while two smaller bedrooms share a compartmented hall bath.

Main floor — 1,385 sq. ft.
Basement — 1,385 sq. ft.
Garage — 576 sq. ft.

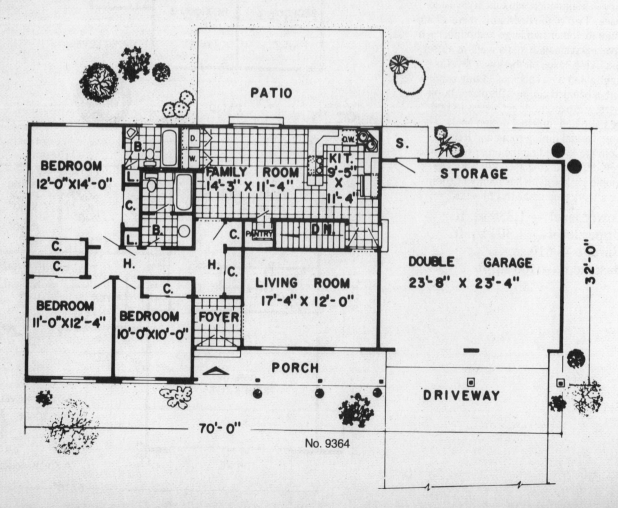

No. 9364

Dignified Design Opens to Family Style Floor Plan

No. 10496

Four spacious bedrooms are arranged on the upper level of this plan so that privacy is maintained without any wasted space. Two of the bedrooms share a bath while the other two large bedrooms each have a private bath and a walk-in closet. The living space on the lower level is highlighted by a spacious family room with a beamed ceiling, fireplace, bookcases, wetbar and direct access to both the patio and informal dining nook. The more formal dining room and living room are located on the other side of the well-designed U-shaped kitchen. The double garage even has plenty of room for a workshop and extra bicycles.

Lower level — 1,330 sq. ft.
Upper level — 1,301 sq. ft.
Garage — 610 sq. ft.
Basement — 765 sq. ft.

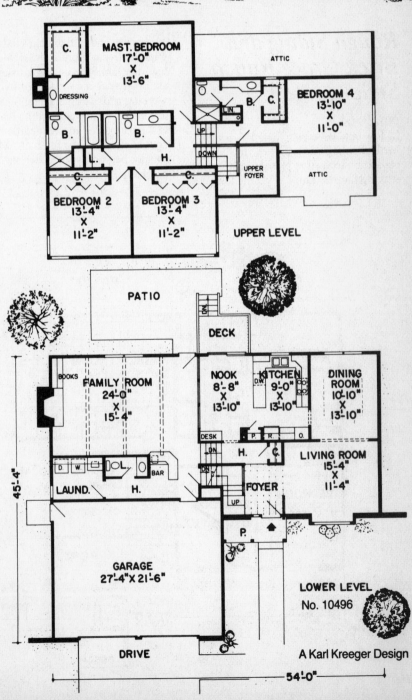

MAST. BEDROOM
17'-0" X 13'-6"

C.

DRESSING

ATTIC

BEDROOM 4
13'-10" X 11'-0"

B.

B.

LIN.

B. C.

UP

DOWN

UPPER FOYER

ATTIC

H.

BEDROOM 2
13'-4" X 11'-2"

BEDROOM 3
13'-4" X 11'-2"

UPPER LEVEL

PATIO

DECK

BOOKS

FAMILY ROOM
24'-0" X 15'-4"

NOOK
8'-8" X 13'-10"

KITCHEN
9'-0" X 13'-10"

DINING ROOM
10'-10" X 13'-10"

DESK

H.

LIVING ROOM
15'-4" X 11'-4"

D W L BAR

LAUND.

H.

FOYER

UP

P.

GARAGE
27'-4" X 21'-6"

45'-4"

DRIVE

54'-0"

LOWER LEVEL
No. 10496

A Karl Kreeger Design

Two Fireplaces Featured

No. 10431

It's the little details that add interest and character to a design and set it apart from others. The master bedroom on the right balances the living room on the left (both with bay windows), giving the front elevation a feeling of symmetry. The front entry between them features double doors flanked by side lights. The living room, decorated by a raised hearth fireplace, flows through a graceful arch doorway to a dining room beyond. The family woodchopper will be kept busy supplying this fireplace and an additional one in the family room, with wood. Every nook and cranny in the floor plan seems to boast of storage and closet space or an added extra such as a bar in the family room or pantry right outside the kitchen.

First floor — 2,108 sq. ft.
Second floor — 509 sq. ft.
Garage — 532 sq. ft.

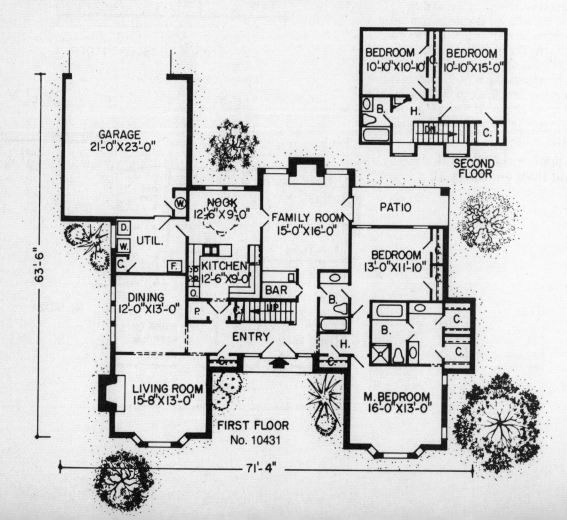

Focus on Family Activities

No. 90124

The whole family will enjoy the arrangement of this traditionally styled three bedroom home. Family and guests alike will be drawn to the cozy family room that opens onto the patio. The warm fireplace and beamed ceiling spread their charm to the adjacent kitchen, which easily serves the counter area and the formal dining room. The mudroom entrance is made even more practical by combining it with laundry facilities. A 3/4 bath complete the first floor. Each of the 3 roomy bedrooms on the second floor has ample closet space with the master suite enjoying a large walk-in.

First floor — 1,080 sq. ft.
Second floor — 868 sq. ft.

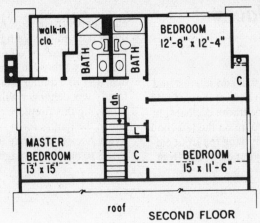

roof   SECOND FLOOR

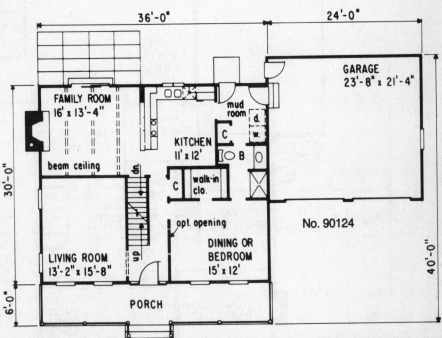

No. 90124

Angled Living Room Draws Attention

No. 10427

The exciting prospects of this home will satisfy those with an appreciation of beauty and design. Each area is singularly attractive as well as functioning with other rooms to create an appealing whole. Rising two stories to skylights above, an entry gallery routes traffic patterns to living and dining areas. The homemaker will find the step-saving kitchen a delight with its sunny corner sink, its location only steps away from the bay-windowed formal dining room, and the convenience of the nearby nook and pantry.

First floor — 2,300 sq. ft.
Second floor — 578 sq. ft.
Garage — 516 sq. ft.

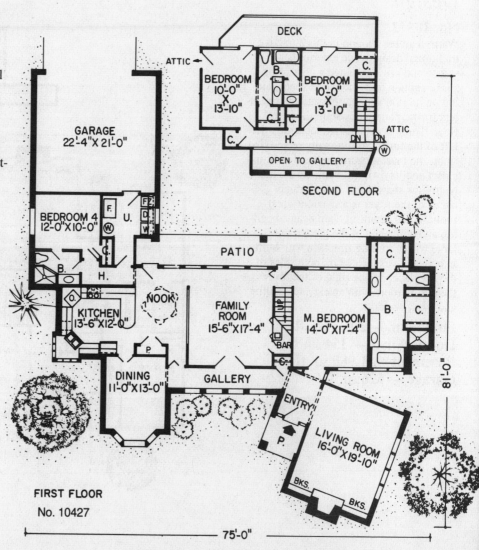

BRUCE LEBOLD

Charming Traditional Design

No. 10572

Warm features abound in this attractive traditional design. The exterior has a stucco and brick frontage with a wood shake shingle roof and wood veneer siding on its side and rear elevations. Excellent traffic patterns exist on the first floor. Three bedrooms are located to the left of the foyer. Additionally on the first floor, the master bedroom has a walk-in closet and its own full bath. Two other bedrooms share a full bath. Straight ahead of the foyer is a spacious great room with a beautiful open beamed ceiling and at the end of the great room is a large wood-burning fireplace with built-in bookshelves located on both sides of the fireplace. To the right of the foyer is the dining room with an elevated ceiling and a bay window.

First floor — 2,022 sq. ft.
Dormer plan — 354 sq. ft.2
Basement — 1,980 sq. ft.
Garage — 526 sq. ft.

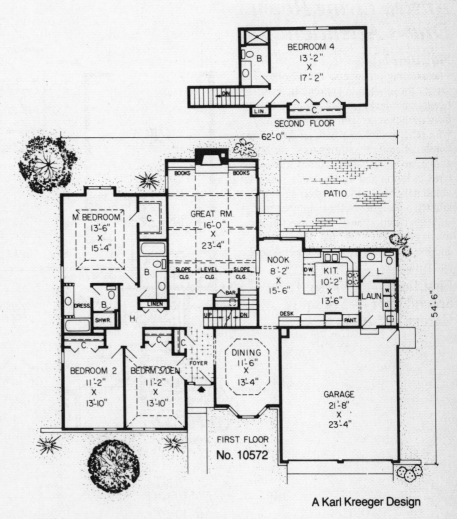

A Karl Kreeger Design

To Order Toll Free
1-800-235-5700

Connecticut, Alaska, Hawaii, and foreign
residents call 1-203-632-0500

handy
materials list
available
for most
home designs

Put Over 80 Years of Experience to Work for You

Get Results Fast

Your complete, accurate Garlinghouse blueprints contain all the information your builder needs to begin construction on your custom home right away. You'll speed every step of the construction of your new home because each detail of construction and materials is already worked out for you and your builder.

Save Time and Money

There's no cheaper way to have the home you've always wanted than our custom blueprints. You pay only a fraction of the original design cost by a respected architect or professional designer. And, our years of experience go into every plan to save you costly mistakes and delays during construction.

Speed Construction, Avoid Delay

You'll speed every step of construction by ordering enough sets of blueprints for the job. Experience shows that 8 sets is best. Once you begin building, everyone seems to need a set. Your lending institution, local building authority, and general contractor each need a set.

And, of course, all the subcontractors will need a set once work is underway . . . the foundation contractor, the framing carpenters, the plumbing contractor, the heating and air conditioning contractor, the electrical contractor, the insulation contractor, the drywall or plastering contractor, the finish carpenters, etc.

While some sets can be handed down as work progresses, you'll avoid delays by having enough sets and eliminate worry about sets being lost or ruined on the job. You'll get faster and better results with the standard 8-set construction package.

Save Even More with a Materials List

Save even more with a materials list for your plan. This helpful list gives the dimensions and specifications of all materials needed to build your home (except for small hardware like nails and screws and the heating/air conditioning, electrical, and plumbing materials which vary according to your local building codes).

With this valuable list, you'll get faster and more accurate bids from your suppliers and avoid paying for unnecessary materials and waste. A materials list is available for most of our plans. Ask when you order.

Here's What You Get

Every set of our complete, accurate blueprints contains everything you need to begin building:

- *Front, rear, and both side views of the house (elevations)*
- *Floor plans for all levels*
- *Foundation plan*
- *Roof plan*
- *Typical wall sections (cross sectional slices through the home)*
- *Kitchen and bathroom cabinet details*
- *Fireplace details (where applicable)*
- *Stair details (where applicable)*
- *Plot plan*
- *Locations of electrical fixtures and components*
- *Specifications and contract form*
- *Energy Conservation Specifications Guide*
- *Complete materials list (only if ordered and available)*

Add a Personal Touch to Your Home

Your custom dream home can be as wonderful as you want. Easy modifications, such as minor non-structural changes and simple building material substitutions, can be made by any competent builder without the need for blueprint revisions. However, if you are considering making major changes to

188

Zoned for Privacy

No. 91217

Don't worry about compromising your privacy in this one-level beauty. This plan is zoned to keep active and quiet areas separate. Step down from the foyer to a wide-open living room that flows into the formal dining room. Cathedral ceilings add to the spacious feeling that continues throughout active areas with an island kitchen open to the breakfast room. French doors lead from the kitchen to a screened porch, a nice warm-weather spot for your morning coffee. Down a hallway off the living room lie three bedrooms, each with a unique character. Notice how closets provide a separation from the bustle of active areas. And, with two full baths, even the morning rush shouldn't be a problem in this house.

Living area — 1,811 sq. ft.
Screened porch — 121 sq. ft.
Garage — 437 sq. ft.

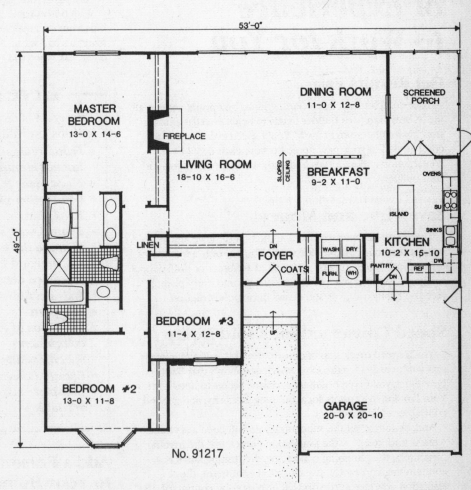

No. 91217

Builder's Library

The books on this page were written with the professional home builder in mind. They are all comprehensive information sources for contractors or for those beginners who wish to build like contractors.

2518. Build Your Own Home An authoritative guide on how to be your own general contractor. This book goes through the step-by-step process of building a house with special emphasis on the business aspects such as financing, scheduling, permits, insurance, and more. Furthermore, it gives you an understanding of what to expect out of your various subcontractors so that you can properly orchestrate their work. 112 pp.; Holland House (paperback) **$12.95**

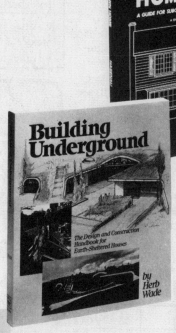

▶ **2600. Building Underground** This has been compiled on earth sheltered homes, built all over North America—homes that are spacious, attractive and comfortable in every way. These homes are more energy efficient than above ground houses. Physical security, low operating costs, and noise reduction further enhance their attractiveness. 304 pp.; 85 photos; 112 illus.; Rodale Press (paperback) **$14.95**

from the Leading Publishers in the Do-It-Yourself Industry!!!

◀ **2596. How To Get It Built** No matter how small or how large your construction project is, building will be easier with this informative guidebook. This text was prepared for people involved in building on a non-professional basis. Guidelines have been carefully prepared to follow step-by-step construction-cost savings methods. Written by an architect/contractor, this book offers home construction owners the planning, construction and cost saving solutions to his own building needs. 238 pp.; over 300 illus.; (paperback) Hashagen **$18.00**

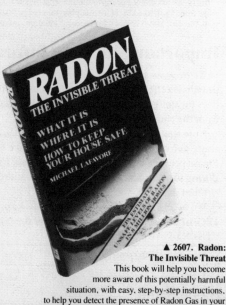

▶ **2508. Modern Plumbing** All aspects of plumbing installation, service, and repair are presented here in illustrated, easy-to-follow text. This book contains all the information needed for vocational competence, including the most up-to-date tools, materials, and practices. 300 pp.; over 700 illus.; Goodheart-Willcox (hardcover) **$17.60**

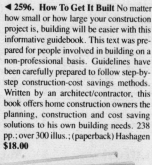

▲ **2607. Radon: The Invisible Threat** This book will help you become more aware of this potentially harmful situation, with easy, step-by-step instructions, to help you detect the presence of Radon Gas in your home. Also included is a simple test that could prevent your home from becoming a victim of this environmental hazard. 224 pp.; Rodale (paperback) **$12.95**

your design, we strongly recommend that you seek the services of an architect or professional designer. Even these expensive professional services will cost less with our complete, detailed plans as a starting point.

Our Custom Design Staff may be able to help you, too, for a very reasonable hourly charge. One advantage of choosing our staff is that we make changes directly to our original drawings and give you a new, complete set of blueprints. Other architects can only attach modified drawings to our originals, which can be more confusing and time consuming for your builder. Call us for more information. Please note that we can make no modifications to #90,000 series plans.

Discover Reverse Plans

You may find that a particular house would suit your taste or fit your lot better if it were "reversed." A reverse plan turns the design end-for-end. That is, if the garage is shown on the left side and the bedrooms on the right, the reverse plan will place the garage on the right side and the bedrooms on the left. To see quickly how a design will look in reverse, hold your book in front of a mirror.

The dimensions and lettering for some Garlinghouse reverse plans are corrected to be right reading on the reversed plan. When this is not the case, one mirror image, reversed set (with "backwards" lettering and dimensions) is provided as a master guide for you and your builder. The remaining sets are then sent as shown in our catalog for ease in reading the lettering and dimensions and marked "REVERSE" with a special stamp to eliminate confusion. (Available only on multiple set orders.)

Prices are effective 1987 and subject to change without notice.

Price Schedule

One Complete Set of Blueprints	$125.00
Minimum Construction Package (5 sets)	$170.00
Standard Construction Package (8 sets)	$200.00
Each Additional Set Ordered With One of the Above Packages	$20.00
Materials List (with plan order only)	$15.00

Builders: ask about our reproducible sepia mylars for professional use. Prices range from $340 to $475. Note that plans numbered 90,000 and above are not available. Call 203-632-0500 for more information and to order.

Important Shipping Information

We process and ship your order within 72 hours of receipt, usually via UPS. Then, it normally takes another 5 to 7 working days for delivery. Please allow 10 working days for delivery from the time we receive your order.

Note that UPS will deliver only to street addresses and rural route delivery boxes and not to Post Office Box numbers. Please print your complete street address. If no one is home during the day, you may use your work address to insure prompt delivery.

We **MUST** ship First Class Mail to Alaska or Hawaii, APO, FPO, or a Post Office box. Please note the higher cost for First Class Mail.

Domestic Shipping	
UPS Ground Service	$5.75
First Class Mail	$7.75

For fastest service, use your **Visa or Mastercard** and call our Toll Free number. If you are in a special hurry, we offer ultra-

fast delivery for an additional charge. Ask for details when you place your order.

International Orders and Shipping

If you are ordering from outside the United States, please note that your check, money order, or international money transfer **must be payable in U.S. currency.**

Also note that due to the extremely long delays involved with surface mail, we ship all international orders via Air Parcel Post. Please refer to the schedule below for the mailing charge on your order and substitute this amount instead of the usual mailing charge for domestic orders.

International Shipping	One set	Multiple sets
Canada	$ 5.75	$ 9.75
Mexico & Caribbean nations	$16.50	$39.50
All other nations	$18.50	$50.00

for fastest service . . .
Order Toll Free
1-800-235-5700
Connecticut, Alaska, Hawaii, and foreign residents call 1-203-632-0500
Please have your credit card and order form ready when you call

The Garlinghouse Co., P.O. Box 1717, Middletown, CT 06457

Blueprint Order Form

Please send me: code no. 20019

☐ One Complete Set of Blueprints ($125.00)
☐ Minimum Construction Package: five sets ($170.00)
☐ Standard Construction Package: eight sets ($200.00)

Plan no. _____   ☐ as shown   ☐ reversed

Cost of Blueprints. . . . .$ _____
_____ Additional Set(s) $20.00 each. . . . .$ _____
        with original order
Materials List ($15.00 per order). . . . . . .$ _____
Shipping Charges (see charts) . . . . $ _____
Tax* . . . .$ _____
        *Kansas Residents Add 5% Sales Tax
        Connecticut Residents Add 7.5% Sales Tax
Total Amount Enclosed . . . . $ _____

Purchaser hereby agrees that the home plan construction drawings being purchased will not be used for the construction of more than one single dwelling, and that these drawings will not be reproduced, either in whole or in part, by any means whatsoever.

Charge my Order to: ☐ Mastercard   ☐ Visa

Card No. ☐☐☐☐☐☐☐☐☐☐☐☐☐☐☐☐☐☐☐☐

Exp.
Date _____ Signature _____

Name _____
                    (please print)

Address _____

City & State _____ Zip _____

Daytime Telephone No. (_____) _____

Send your Check or Money Order to:
The Garlinghouse Company
34 Industrial Park Place, P.O. Box 1717
Middletown, Connecticut 06457

Builder's Library order form

code no.
20026

Yes! send me the following books:

book order no.	price
_____	$ _____
_____	$ _____
_____	$ _____
_____	$ _____
_____	$ _____
_____	$ _____

Postage & handling (one book only) $ 1.75
Add 50¢ postage & handling
  for each additional book $ _____
Canada add $1.50 per book $ _____
Resident sales tax: Kansas (5%) $ _____
            Connecticut (7.5%) $ _____
           TOTAL ENCLOSED $ _____

No C.O.D. orders accepted; U.S. funds only.
prices subject to change without notice

My Shipping Address is:
(please print)

Name _____
Address _____
City _____
State _____ Zip _____

Send your order to:

(With check or money order enclosed)

The Garlinghouse Company
34 Industrial Park Place
P.O. Box 1717
Middletown, Connecticut 06457

For Faster Service . . .
CHARGE IT!   (203) 632-0500

☐ MasterCard   ☐ Visa

Card # |_|_|_|_|_|_|_|_|_| Exp. Date _____

Signature _____

192

▼ **2604. The Low Maintenance House** At last, an idea-packed book that will save you thousands of hours on home maintenance. It's an essential planning guide for anyone building a home. Discover new as well as time-tested techniques and products for cutting down the time, and slashing the money you spend to clean and repair your home . . . from roof to basement, from front yard to backyard garden. This book will earn its price, and your thanks, over and over again. 314 pp.; Rodale (hardback) **$19.95**

▲ **2605. Contracting Your Home** With over 150 illustrations, this guide offers many suggestions and ideas on contracting your own home. Many forms you can copy and re-use are provided, giving checklists and a glossary of terms used by the professionals, as well as all the necessary estimating forms. 279 pp.; Betterway Publications (paperback) **$18.95**

▼ **2608. Cut Your Electric Bill in Half** With assistance from this book, you may be able to cut your future electric bills by up to 80%! With tables outlining the effective use of all your home appliances and recommendations for money-saving appliances, this book is a MUST for the budget-conscious household. 160 pp.; Rodale (paperback) **$9.95**

▲ **2542. Designing and Building a Solar House** Written by one of America's foremost authorities on solar architecture. It is a practical "how-to" guide that clearly demonstrates the most sensible ways to marry good house design with contemporary solar technology. Included is a thorough discussion of both "active" and "passive" solar systems, and even a listing of today's leading solar homes. 288 pp.; 400 illus.; Garden Way (paperback) **$15.95**

▼ **2610. The Backyard Builder** Here is a step-by-step guide for over 150 projects for the gardener and homeowner, accompanied by over 100 photos, 400 illustrations, materials lists and shopping guides. You are sure to find many useful, attractive projects that the entire family can help with. 656 pp.; Rodale (hardcover) **$21.95**

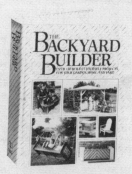

▲ **2606. Building Fences** With emphasis on function and style, this guide to a wide variety of fence-building is a solid how-to book. With easy-to-read instructions, and plenty of illustrations, this book is a must for the professional and the do-it-yourselfer. 188 pp.; Williamson Publishing (paperback) **$13.95**

▲ **2546. Blueprint Reading for Construction** This combination text and workbook shows and tells how to read residential, commercial, and light industrial prints. With an abundance of actual drawings from industry, you learn step by step about each component of a set of blueprints, including even cost estimating. 336 pp.; Goodheart-Willcox (spiral bound) **$18.40**

▲ **2570. Modern Masonry** Everything you will ever need to know about concrete, masonry, and brick, is included in this book. Forms construction, concrete reinforcement, proper foundation construction, and bricklaying are among the topics covered in step-by-step detail. An excellent all-round reference and guide. 256 pp.; 700 illus.; Goodheart-Willcox (hardcover) **$17.00**

▼ **2514. The Underground House Book** For anyone seriously interested in building and living in an underground home, this book tells it all. Aesthetic considerations, building codes, site planning, financing, insurance, planning and decorating considerations, maintenance costs, soil, excavation, landscaping, water considerations, humidity control, and specific case histories are among the many facets of underground living dealt with in this publication. 208 pp.; 140 illus.; Garden Way (paperback) **$10.95**

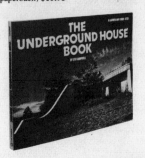

▼ **2504. Architecture, Residential Drawing and Design** An excellent text that explains all the fundamentals on how to create a complete set of construction drawings. Specific areas covered include proper design and planning considerations, foundation plans, floor plans, elevations, stairway details, electrical plans, plumbing plans, etc. 492 pp.; over 800 illus.; Goodheart-Willcox (hardcover) **$22.00**

▲ **2510. Modern Carpentry** A complete guide to the "nuts and bolts" of building a home. This book explains all about building materials, framing, trim work, insulation, foundations, and much more. A valuable text and reference guide. 492 pp.; over 1400 illus.; Goodheart-Willcox (hardcover) **$22.00**

▲ **2506. House Wiring Simplified** This book teaches all the fundamentals of modern house wiring; shows how it's done with easy-to-understand drawings. A thorough guide to the materials and practices for safe, efficient installation of home electrical systems. 176 pp.; 384 illus.; Goodheart-Willcox (hardcover) **$9.20**

▼ **2544. Solar Houses** An examination of solar homes from the standpoint of lifestyle. This publication shows you through photographs, interviews, and practical information, what a solar lifestyle involves, how owners react to it, and what the bottom-line economics are. Included are 130 floor plans and diagrams which give you a clear idea of how various "active" and "passive" solar systems work. 160 pp.; 370 illus. Pantheon (paperback) **$9.95**

▼ **2592. How to Design & Build Decks & Patios** Learn how to create decks and patios to suit every type of lot and lifestyle. This fully illustrated source book includes detailed information on design and construction as well as special charts on building and paving materials. Full color, 112 pp.; Ortho (paperback) **$6.95**

▲ **2609. Kitchens** Gather your family around you in your new kitchen, with tips from the professionals in the industry, as well as 105 color photos to help you design your new kitchen. With recommendations on a wide variety of related topics, even the casual reader is sure to find exciting new ideas for their kitchen. 160 pp.; Rodale (paperback) **$12.95**

▲ **2612. Baths** With charts and illustrations provided, BATHS gives tips on new storage ideas, suggestions on whirlpools and saunas, and a tour of 30 of the best-designed baths in the United States. Assistance is provided in the form of addresses of leading manufacturers and helpful organizations, to aid you in the remodeling of your bath. 154 pp.; Rodale (paperback) **$12.95**

▼ **2611. Tile It Up! Plumb It Up!** Using the many illustrations and the easy steps included in this valuable book, you will be able to work just like the professionals. This book provides step-by-step instructions on plumbing and tiling, enabling the do-it-yourselfer to complete these projects with a minimum of time providing maximum results. 43 pp.; XS Books (paperback) **$6.95**

▼ **2516. Building Consultant** The new home buyer's bible to home construction. This encyclopedia of home building explains in comprehensive detail about all the various elements that go into a completed house. It enables you to deal with the construction of your new home in a meaningful way that will avoid costly errors, whether you use a contractor or build it yourself. 188 pp.; Holland House (paperback) **$12.95**